Praise for *Zombies to Zeal*
Reawaken the Human Spiri

MW00884140

"To know the author is to love her; to read the author is to be inspired by her. DJ is a unique blend of head and heart, leader and storyteller. If you've ever felt dispirited on or off the job, this book's for you. DJ's uplifting insights will resonate with you and motivate you to come alive so that everyone you deal with comes alive too."

- Sam Horn, author of *POP!* and *Got Your Attention?*

"Chock-full of inspiring stories and practical tips, *Zombies to Zealots* reveals why people become disengaged 'zombies' and shares the secret of how to bring them back to life. This playful, memorable book is a must-read for leaders looking to not only improve engagement but ignite the full passion and creativity of their teams."

- Stephan Mardyks and David Covey, SMCOV Co-Founders

"DJ Mitsch has years of experience helping leaders wake up employees who have either checked-out or drowned in their resentment. She has translated her wisdom in *Zombies to Zealots* with heartfelt inspiration, delightful lightness and starkly honest truth. Read this book a few times and then carry it with you to give your spirit it's daily spark of life.

- Marcia Reynolds, PsyD, author of *The Discomfort Zone: How Leaders Turn Difficult Conversations into Breakthroughs*

ZOMBIES
TO
ZEALOTS

REAWAKEN THE HUMAN SPIRIT AT WORK!

DARELYN 'DJ' MITSCH

BALBOA.
PRESS

A DIVISION OF HAY HOUSE

Balboa Press books may be ordered through booksellers or by contacting:

Balboa Press
A Division of Hay House
1663 Liberty Drive
Bloomington, IN 47403
www.balboapress.com
1 (877) 407-4847

Because of the dynamic nature of the Internet, any web addresses or links contained in this book may have changed since publication and may no longer be valid. The views expressed in this work are solely those of the author and do not necessarily reflect the views of the publisher, and the publisher hereby disclaims any responsibility for them.

The author of this book does not dispense medical advice or prescribe the use of any technique as a form of treatment for physical, emotional, or medical problems without the advice of a physician, either directly or indirectly. The intent of the author is only to offer information of a general nature to help you in your quest for emotional and spiritual well-being. In the event you use any of the information in this book for yourself, which is your constitutional right, the author and the publisher assume no responsibility for your actions.

Any people depicted in stock imagery provided by Thinkstock are models, and such images are being used for illustrative purposes only. Certain stock imagery © Thinkstock.

Print information available on the last page.

ISBN: 978-1-5043-5640-4 (sc)
ISBN: 978-1-5043-5642-8 (hc)
ISBN: 978-1-5043-5641-1 (e)

Library of Congress Control Number: 2016906877

Balboa Press rev. date: 07/13/2016

Contents

Beth Gordon

Bob Spetrini

Brian Dubaj

Colleen Dodson

Craig Flanagan

Daina Trout

Doug Buriani

Ed Mimikos

Erica Lembo

Gregory Doherty

Heather Evans

Jennifer Bornhoeft

John Vincere

Jose Michael Alvarez

Kristi D'Errico

Lance Griffin

Lauren Botticelli

Mike Myers

Reggie Gatewood

Rich Davis

R. Scott Fellers

Roger Marsh

Sandra Birckhead

Scott Kapeller

Stacy Lindley

Stephanie Rester

Susie Kelleher

Victor Gairani

With Heartfelt Gratitude

For Anne Whitaker

And

The Change Agents!

How to Read or Use This Book

Zombies to Zealots calls on you to embrace the concept of *embodiment*: living and embracing your truth with your entire being, including your heart, your brain, your "guts," and, most important, your *spirit*.

This book is an embodied collection of insights and stories from my work with amazing people, both clients and colleagues. It reframes contrasts between the disembodied, disjointed mind-sets of workplace knuckle draggers and those who embark on heroic journeys to come back to life. The last chapter is a nod to those who risk changing cultures to create the ideal—organizations filled with passionate, exuberant, workplace zealots.

Zombies to Zealots is soul food and consumable for even those with jammed-up gray matter and a short attention span. It does not matter where you begin or end. You can start at the beginning or just read the chapter that resonates for you. Play with the ideas within. Let the words speak to you as you consider the four paths back into the light of conscious connection.

Introduction

Why I Wrote *Zombies to Zealots*

These days, leaders and their human resources partners are urgently questioning how to get people to engage fully in daily endeavors. The chaos people experience in organizational change, the amount of information poured into their brains, and, the sense of identity loss or any lack of hope for success in many organizations has created *zombie teams*. The world's largest and most successfully traded companies are full of disengaged, cynical members who leave weekly meetings to mindlessly follow orders out of fear of consequences, questioning if they will ever be or do enough. After these meetings, they gather at the local watering hole to commiserate, trying to decide what's next. Not only are people weary, disheartened, and shutting down, they are disconnected from their truth and creative spirit. And when I say *people,* I am including the many leaders who drive daily mandates in ways that they can't actually stomach. It is high time that we revolutionize the way we work and lead and that we liberate people to bring their best contributions to each day. Through my work as a coach, I have witnessed some things I felt were worth sharing, beginning with what it means to be an enthusiastic leader—a regular-person zealot—and to call your spirit back into the work you do. Among those I've been privileged to coach are the people I mention on the dedication page.

Anne's Story: A Revolutionary Zealot Leader

Let me introduce you to the remarkable leader, change agent, and fired-up human being mentioned on the dedication page. From the time Anne was old enough to speak, her mantra was, "I can do it… myself!" Her mother tells stories of Anne crawling into her own crib at night when she was just over a year old, refusing to be lifted into her bed by anyone who stood taller. That independent spirit has been with her since she landed on the planet, just as your inner spark has been there with you.

As Anne made her way through high school, she faced the typical teenage challenges and disappointments that helped shape what I call the *inner revolutionary (aka rebel)*—that part of us all that typically surfaces around the time we are able to climb into our own cribs, when we want to just do everything ourselves. That spirit within gets louder at age 13 and stays with us, a captive force pacing inside of us, until we acknowledge its voice and pay attention to its power in our lives. Our inner rebel is that part of us that says *no* and aids us in standing up for ourselves when we most need to. We all share this archetype to some degree, although many push it way down into their gut instead of heeding its wisdom. Recognizing all the aspects of your personality, especially this rebel, can give you the power of choosing when it serves you, if you figure out how to work with it.

Anne was an avid ball player from age five through middle and high school, until she was cut from the team her freshman year in high school. She admits she was devastated when the coach didn't call her name for the shortstop position she had played most of her life. Her dad found her in tears later that day. When he asked her what happened, she wept, "I am too slow. I play the wrong position for a left hander. I am just not good enough."

Her Dad, whom Anne says rarely raised his voice, grabbed her shoulder and said, "Don't ever say you are not good enough. YOU are enough!" Then he said, "If you really want this, you CAN do it and I will help you. You are going to have to work hard, hustle even more than ever, and get stronger. We will do this together. Are you willing to do the work?" Her answer was absolutely "yes." She was partly stunned by her Dad's reaction, yet also incredibly motivated by the notion of this possibility.

So her father, who drove a bread truck for 47 years, getting up at 2:00 am every day to load his truck, then working 14-16 hour days, helped Anne overcome the challenge of being a left-handed shortstop and catcher (her back-up position). He helped her build a workout plan to get faster—to learn to turn quicker to complete her throws to first base. He took that one thing that she really wanted to do—play ball and, most importantly, be part of the team, leveraged her hustle, and convinced her that "she was enough." Anne tells the story of her Dad's belief in her and his personal sacrifice often with tear-filled eyes. It is abundantly clear that he is her hero and a huge part of the person she is today as she stands confidently knowing, even in the toughest of times, that "she is enough."

Whether it was fortune or fate, it turned out that mid-season one of the shortstops on the team broke her ankle. Anne often quips, when she tells this story, that some say she may have been "hit by a bread truck." Anne humbly talks about how her teammates of ten years asked the coach to let her try out mid-season for the shortstop opening. They knew she had been practicing on her own and they also knew that while Anne wasn't the star player, the team was better when she was there.

So the coach allowed Anne to try out to fill the spot, and this time she made the team. That season, she played better than ever before as she gained new confidence, but most importantly the team played better.

This story speaks to Anne's tenacity and resilience. Privileged to have been Anne's coach and a business partner for some amazing work over the past 17 years, I wanted to share some of the lessons and victories from our journey together, with this central idea—YOU are enough. When was the last time you felt that way? Has anyone ever said that to you? If not, read on. You will find clarity and hope within these pages. The endless striving and sense of frustration that leaves most people disheartened can be changed when you understand and take back your personal power. You will have to do some work to get there, but as the pages in this book will soon remind you, work and play can actually become the same game.

A Quick Background

Through Pyramid Resource Group—the corporate coaching company my husband and I launched in 1993—our team has coached many amazing people like Anne. In fact we have coached over 5,000 leaders and more teams than we can count to lead differently by reenergizing and reengaging their teams, creating for us an informal (and sometimes formal) body of research from which we have gathered themes. We've learned so much in the process, much of it shared in this book.

One theme is that people everywhere really want the same things: significant and meaningful work, the love of family and friends, and the ability to make a positive impact or difference in the world. In addition, we all want the freedom to play, create, and have fun again! Fun is a core value for every soul we encounter. By *fun,* I mean simply the joy derived from doing something that matters—not hanging upside down from a tree on a ropes course, although I have done that and it is indeed fun. Fun comes from working together with other people to do something so invigorating and energizing that we forget we are working. Fun is a big missing link in engaging the hearts and minds of people to play bigger.

I wanted to share some observations from our work about why people are becoming so disengaged, why this zombie outbreak is becoming an epidemic that needs to be addressed, and why it is time to reawaken the human spirit at work, along with some ways to do that. I wrote about zombies and zealots because it was a most fun way of communicating some pretty serious stuff!

I wrote this book because now is the time for humanity to fully awaken to our power. We are spiritual beings in human form, and I believe that we have a simple mission to learn to love each other, to go to Earth school, and to evolve; we do so by elevating the way we work and play together on this gem of a planet—and there is a growing sense of urgency in the world to clean up our collective act.

I wrote this book because humanity is amazing and resourceful and creative, and we can choose happiness every day and change the things that are not working. We have the power to do that. If I could give you one gift, it would be to grab your shoulder, raise my voice and tell you, "YOU are enough." If I could give you one message about being born on the planet at this time and space, it would be this:

> You are powerful. You are enough. You are perfect. We welcome you to this place and we cannot wait to see what you do next! You came to play an extraordinary game here, with us, to help lift mankind into a new level of consciousness. This is your time to shine. Let's play together—full out—and create the future, hand in hand.

Ready?

Zombie or Zealot?

Here's the scary truth.

The Zombie Apocalypse is upon us, signaling that this is our time to awaken the others and get moving from darkness and daily despair back into the light.

A viral epidemic of numbing out is taking place in most organizations, which have been overrun by people who have lost their inner spark, motivation, and zeal for their work. Silently trudging through the hallways, stumbling hollow-eyed through the workweek, many people have sold their souls for a paycheck and are experiencing little meaning on the job. You know who these zombies are and maybe can even relate to them. It really doesn't matter what positions they hold. They share their doom, despair, and misery—sometimes shouting or mumbling directions so other people also become dazed and confused—in ways that contaminate or infect their teams and the larger organization.

Recently, I received e-mails with raised flags and cries for help from executive and human resources clients I've coached over the years in global organizations that are navigating big changes in their strategies. They are sensing the zombie apocalypse, even if they don't have a name for it, as evidenced by the language in their e-mails:

"Ugh! It's like the walking dead around here given the news last week!"

"Our teams are being blown apart and disembodied weekly."

"Well the new company that acquired us is saying all the right things, but their actions are not congruent. They are actually rude and dismissive of all the things we have done to build a company worthy of their attention.

"Welcome to this week's 'Soul-Sucking Sh#& Show'"

"I have no connection to the people around here anymore. I sit in the cafeteria, staring out at a sea of people I don't know, and I am hesitant to connect because the emotional costs are too high. I know that some of them will be on the cut list next week."

"It's like Groundhog Day around here. Same old crap from the same old sources."

That kind of commentary is not unusual these days. These people, like you, are working like crazy, asked to do more and more, feeling like they can never do or be enough. Most of you don't know what *enough* really means, but you know in your gut it includes a brain drain, and you've recently noticed that your feet are dragging and many of the people around you are sleepwalking through the day. That's how this contagious virus of the disembodied works. It does not discriminate. It hits executives, leaders, and employees at every level. Even if you are still happy or in a new job and are not a party to predatory acts, you can see it happening around you and fear you may become infected!

If you feel like you have become a working zombie, you're not alone. A 2014 Gallup Workforce study found that seven out of ten workers, a full 70 percent of the U.S. workforce, identify themselves as disengaged, with only 30 percent reporting that they are actively engaging in fulfilling and meaningful work.[1] With the Bureau of Labor Statistics reporting that the U.S. workforce, as of November 2015, is around 149 million workers,[2] that means that over *104 million* workers—your friends, your family, your colleagues—are not happy. Many are not giving their best effort because they don't see any link between their work and meaning. They're not contributing their wealth of talent and resources because they don't see the point of doing so. This is one of the biggest problems any company or executive faces.

No one takes a job with the intention of being miserable and dissatisfied. The fact that the majority of workers do end up being so unhappy begs a couple of questions:

1. What are we all going to do in response to this epidemic?
2. What can an individual—what can you—do now?

One option is to personally shift your perspective and get your groove back at work: You can pursue the right work and become a change agent—a person who risks courageous acts of enthusiasm and helps to unleash possibility every day—right where you are now. Or you can run and hide as you await the next round of mergers, take a package, and be on your merry one-year hiatus while you retool to take another job, where you will encounter these same people and situations.

That's right: The second option is only a temporary solution, because if you look around, most organizations have the same types of people, regardless of what products or services they offer. And the workforce engagement studies are global, so if you are considering running away to another country, take a look at the unemployment rates and the engagement scores there first. No matter where you sign on for your next job, you are going to bump into workplace zombies. They are, indeed, everywhere. When you think of it this way, reengagement, or finding your zeal where you are now, becomes an option worth considering.

My observations and research are derived from over twenty years leading a dynamic company of coaches to support leaders to resuscitate historically great and high growth organizations through culture-changing initiatives. We accomplished this in part by challenging leaders to get real—become more authentic—and to focus on energizing people as their key business strategy. Their own heroes' journeys, turnaround efforts, and vulnerabilities inspired me, and it is time to share what I have learned in hopes that doing so will help others find their inner spark and shift from zombie to zealot.

Over the years, we have framed many of the coaching initiatives by challenging our clients to see work as an extraordinary game. In the process, we have found that people everywhere are ready to play such a game and to help drive the changes needed to lift their organizations. They step up, communicate requests instead of complain, and take the lead when it's time. Everywhere we go, that single shift of focus from "work" to "game" has helped to change the water cooler dialogue throughout organizations from "I can't" to "we can" within a few short months.

We have discovered that not only are people ready to get their game on, they are longing for someone to actually listen to them, heed what they say, clarify who they really are, and help them find their way back to life. When they are given these gifts of attention from those around them, especially their leaders, people become excited, working zealots who have a genuine sense that they are in control of their destinies and that they can and are contributing to the organization.

Work and Play: Same Game

The word *work* comes from the Middle English word *weorc,* is related to words like *travail* and *wreak* (as in *havoc*), and was once closely associated with struggle and torture. I hope that doesn't give you comfort.

Work became more commonly used about two hundred years ago to define the shift in energy through the introduction of a change agent in the field of physics. It was a verb that captured the manipulation of energy. Now it is a verb, a noun, an adjective, and central to all of our language, and people assume everyone means the same thing when they talk about work. But do they?

My children attended Montessori schools when they were really young. Montessori teachers interchanged the word *work* with *play,* and each morning and afternoon, my kids took their game boards, puzzles, modeling clay, or art to mats where they would "work" until they were ready to change their projects or lessons. Work and play were the same thing because they were young and impressionable. For my kids and many others, including me, this concept stuck because it is more fun to view our work through the lens of play or creativity. I intentionally interchange *work* with *play* within these pages. I also refer to what we individuals do with our days as "the game of work!" Approaching work as a game allows employees to play with ideas instead of struggling to get it all right. The notion of a game allows for magic in the spaces where stress on performance might otherwise stop workers. We can be lighter. We can be more creative. We can break some stupid rules. We can make up new agreements. We can pretend. We can go for outrageous new goals. We can call it quits when our approach doesn't work anymore. We can morph the game plan. We can own the rules of the game. We can celebrate winning whenever we want to for whatever we deem worthy, because it is our game and it feeds our souls. If this book calls to you, I hope it is because you are ready to play a new and more meaningful game. You know deep inside that to rehumanize work, we all have some work to do together. It is beyond time for a conscious reawakening of the human spirit, that corporeal intelligence that comes from deep within us and that connects us to each other, flowing as an energetic stream of information and master intelligence.

Z2Z Archetypes: *Zombies* and *Zealots*

Once happy people, working zombies ultimately perpetuate fear and breed discontent, dissatisfaction, and passivity, feeding on the brainpower and energy of others. No one is born a zombie. Yet we can all numb out, lose hope, or become infected when we abandon our sense of meaning and purpose. So how do we define Zombie?

> *Working Zombie*: An overworked, dehumanized soul and shell of a once full-of-life human being; one who lost enthusiasm, zeal, and passion for work; an infectious saboteur who has disengaged at work; s/he commiserates with others, fueling tensions, ritualistically sucking the life out of the company. Also known as a 60-80 hour a week sleepwalker who stares at their mobile devices over dinner with family and friends, unable to break away from the tethers of a demanding role.

In contrast to zombies, let's consider those folks who operate from a place of zeal. These exuberant people start from a place of happiness wherever they are, and they show up that way at work. Their workday is not without challenges, but these folks have a sense of purpose that keeps them motivated to work through the challenges, in spite of bullying bosses or frustrating circumstances like having their team consistently blown apart and reconfigured through organizational changes. Zealots are able to find or create meaning in their work. They look for the lead. They look beyond the internal operations and consider the possibility that what they do really matters to other people and the planet. Zealots don't feel trapped or alone at work because they attract and create a community of like-minded others to work alongside them. The fact of the matter is zealed-out employees do have one characteristic in common with zombies: They are contagious. This contagion is the antidote for the ick, and this zeal energizes people in ways that great leaders hope and pray will go viral.

> *Zealot*: A champion for the human spirit. Zealots are passionate, exuberant, courageous human beings; they are contagious enthusiasts who make no distinction between labor and leisure, vocation and avocation, heart's desire and imagination. Masterful in the art of living, they celebrate every scary step, path, and job they take— learning from every experience, relishing the victories, rising to any challenge, and leaving others to decide if they are working or playing. In their experience, it is always both.

Becoming a zealot is not about turning into some uber-enthused activist who jumps up and down on his desk or a stage; instead it is someone like you and me who knows in their heart that they can live and work in a purposeful way. As for those of you who find yourselves in leadership roles, you are now part of the Zombie Rescue team, like it or not. In order to help with the rescue, there are some things we will all need in our Zombie rescue kits. First let's understand and recall some reasons why people slip into this frozen, numbed out discontent.

The Slippery Slope to Becoming a Zombie: Tripping Down Memory Lane

Have you ever stopped to consider the reasons people disengage and become dissatisfied at work? Everyone starts a new job with some level of enthusiasm and hope. Unless they are taking a job to nowhereland just to pay the rent, the job holds some promise that a dream will be fulfilled. But when people experience the chaos of change or feel out of control, they go within and play smaller. When we start out enthused, we can see the challenges, changes and chaos around us as part of the work—things that we include in our daily celebration of life. But when we go over the edge and slide down the slippery slope to zombie, these same challenges, changes, and chaos send us into despair and eventually we smell or help spread the dirt and doom.

Where would you plot yourself right now on the Workplace Energy Scale that follows? Are you somewhere on the curve up or somewhere on the slippery slope down to sleepwalker, brain-sucking zombie?

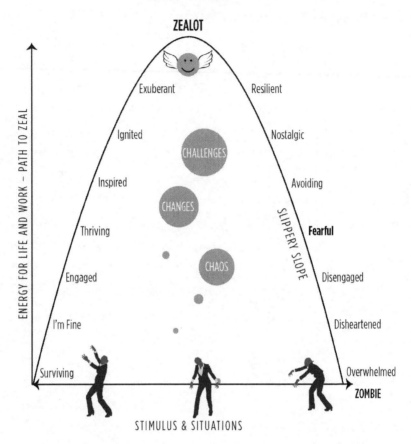

Figure 1. Energy Curve

This curve is not intended to represent a traditional bell curve where the majority of the population falls in the middle with a few straggling outliers on the right and left; rather this curve represents a graphic illustration of the stages we may go through on the way up from zombie at the bottom of the graph on the left side to zealot and the stages we encounter on the way down the slippery slope back toward zombiedom on the right hand side. Note how this scale captures on the left side your energy for work and life. The space in the middle represents the picture of the daily onslaught of *changes, challenges, and chaos.* The right side indicates the states of emotion and reactions to changes, challenges, chaos, and other obstacles when our energy and focus is off. Pick a scenario at work and you can quickly identify your energetic response to it in one of those words, such as avoiding, fearful or disengaged.

Starting at the bottom left side, the scale moves from a status of inertia (zombied) to *surviving* to *exuberant*—to *zealot*—with other stages identifying when our energy and capacity for work increases. Pay special attention to the words "I'm *fine*" as a benchmark. "Fine" is what people typically say when they really aren't fine but cannot muster the energy to say how they really feel. How to move beyond *fine* to *engaged* is a daily endeavor of conscious choices for many people and a conundrum for those who lead them. Moving from *engaged* to *thriving, inspired, ignited,* and *exuberant* requires internal motivations and perspectives, in addition to a dose of positive, external stimulus. Take account of your current status and notice your responses to others when they ask how you are doing today. Then ask yourself, "Where is my energy focused when it comes to my performance?"

Now let's consider how a person can get pulled down the right-hand side of the scale: the *slippery slope.* Most of us start at the top, with being *resilient,* which is the state in which we naturally function to navigate the onslaught of changes and chaos we experience each day. Yet, being resilient at all costs for a stretch of time can send you sliding, especially if it pulls you away from your values, vision, or desires. When you grow weary of being so resilient, you can become nostalgic, reminiscing about the good old days, and move to avoidance and bump up against many of our biggest fears. Those fears include, but are not limited to, how we feel about a lack of resources; loss of position, power, or love; possible death of the ego or physical death; or threats. People easily lose footing when running full force into the workweek. We can all become dispirited as we slide headfirst into overwhelmed and zombie states, without looking up to even question reality, the truth in a situation, or where we got tripped up.

If we are in a healthy state and are engaged, thriving, inspired, and on our way to our happy, zealed-out space, we can bump into challenges, changes and chaos and see hidden possibilities. If we are trying to move back up the slippery slope and encounter similar situations, they can become debilitating. It's as if we are constantly running up a down escalator that has been set on high speed.

The truth is that most people who are now acting zombie-like were once full of vigor and life. Some were zealots for their company or a noble cause served by their company, and some were activist leaders who set out to play a big game on this planet. Over the course of our careers, we've all experienced chaotic and frequent changes in leadership, gotten lost in mergers and acquisitions, worked for ill-equipped or bullying bosses, had insufficient resources, had expectations dashed, sensed a general lack of meaning and vision, and witnessed a disregard for humanity. As a result, we have grown weary, losing hope that things could or would ever change. Becoming compromised and dehumanized has infected otherwise bright and energetic human beings, leaving many as dull versions of their once brilliant selves.

Tracing Our History to Zombiedom

Ever wonder, "How did we get to this place?" The following list is meant to be a home-style buffet of simple observations on how we got to zombiedom today. It doesn't take a genius, a survey, or a body of research to recall these scenarios, yet I thought it might be helpful to trip down this memory lane. These four evolutions of work became a path masses have trod to this current state or precipice.

1. *Assembly Lines and Mechanization.* The invention of the automobile and the industrial revolution presented tradesmen and entrepreneurs with a conundrum: how to consistently replicate products and produce them quickly. Assembly lines were formed and work became routine and somewhat mindless for most people. Mechanization changed and accelerated the industrial revolution. Classes of workers were born: white collar in the office, blue collar on the front line. The trek to zombie land was also born: Assembly workers didn't have to think so much as do. The job was a means to a lifestyle, a home, a car, and tinfoil TV dinners. Even the role of management was about removing blocks to performance for the front line. Management processes were clear and straightforward—black and white—like the TV shows of that era.

2. *Automation and Technology.* Fast forward to the present time. Automation innovated work processes. Robots could do what people did on assembly lines. Computer technology revolutionized how we found, stored, and used information. Around 1993, the Internet created a global framework for the dissemination of information. We could work faster and communicate more broadly and immediately. This platform, in many ways, reconnected people to people and made us curious again. It also gave birth to new commerce. Our children were born technology natives. If one watches what they innately know how to do, it becomes apparent that part of their game of work is recreating the game of work on a platform that evolves and morphs daily. This no-collar workforce created a chasm between their generation and those generations who grew up white or blue collar.

3. *Monitors and Sensor Data Gathering.* The reality is that Big Brother has been and is now watching, and apparently he has company. We understand through our political debates and media microscopes that we have pirates out there waiting to zap us, finding their way into our technology to track us, steal from us, and keep us frozen in fear. This manipulation of our fears and need for safety is used to control how we

react to any change and impacts how we make decisions. We live in abject fear of everything from aging to safety, which drives behaviors as small as what night cream we buy to those as large as how we choose security systems for our homes, or how and when we choose to travel to big cities or foreign countries for business or pleasure. All this observation has resulted in an extraordinary amount of data, which is available to any company on everything from employees' daily habits to consumers' purchasing decisions. That information flow boggles the mind at the same time as it provides food for thought and, perhaps, a small case of the willies. Learning to interpret all of this data takes leaders to a whole new set of management problems, beginning with what to do with all that information on all those people. The focus on continuous improvement in service speed and efficiency is now so paramount that companies emphasize new processes over developing people to lead, inspiring them to contribute and mentoring them to gain confidence, which leaves many workers feeling objectified as a result.

4. *Chaos.* Mergers and acquisitions happen so fast that teams of people who begin projects in the first quarter are blown apart by the middle of second

quarter and are often left leaderless for a while somewhere in the middle. Leaders worth their salt are rapidly promoted or moved to new roles, leaving those who remain behind frozen in place as they await instructions for how to move, get in line for project approvals, and watch for the other giant shoe to fall to herald in the next big change.

We humans are not lazy when we are ignited. When we risk exposure, we will go to great lengths to be our best, explore things, climb mountains, play sports, learn languages, teach others, and otherwise discipline ourselves to achieve greatness. People became robotic mannequins that could perform tasks because that was all that was required of them at a time when many left behind their farms, trades, and crafts to find "real work"—a job they could count on that paid at least minimum wage.

A carrot-and-stick style of managing worked for a very long time in the industries that needed to replicate products so that they attained the same quality day after day. But let's not forget that carrots and sticks were meant for workhorses and mules wearing bridles and bits; that approach worked to move them forward when plowing fields. I can imagine how the line leader who came off the farm thought that was the way to get the assembly going, and I am pretty sure his approach was the first skid mark off the path to happiness for some. Know what I mean?

That approach also led us to eventually numb out as four to five generations took nine-to-five jobs. Workers got up, went to the job, came home, ate dinner, watched TV, and went to bed, only to repeat the same function the next day. That rhythm has lasted for decades, as we found meaning in hobbies—not work—or got lost in reality TV. Seriously, do millions of you really want to be like the Kardashians, rich and famous housewives, or bachelors and bachelorettes? And how can anyone relax watching 24/7 news? News stories feed our fears by hitting us where we are most vulnerable—our money and our sense of safety—by focusing on stock market plunges and peaks, terrorism, and political characters who misbehave. The undercurrent seems intentionally designed to hook us emotionally and keep draining our brains.

In the interest of self-preservation, we have created ways of closing ourselves off or shutting down at the end of a work day. When all that is needed is a shell of a person to do a job—or our goal at work becomes to exert as little energy as possible—why would we put our souls into the effort? Organizational leaders haven't all found their way out of the downward spiral, but I sense they are sincerely seeking new answers. The stimulus–reaction way of working and leading extracted the human spirit from the workplace, and I believe it is fair to say that we all want that experience.

Seven Types of Zombies

People always create their realities in their narratives about themselves. Narratives are stories we tell about our situations and our lives in general. Those who tell happy stories experience more happiness for the most part, even when faced with the same challenges as those who glom on to their fears and miseries. Those who rant, whine, and complain typically tune in to ranting, whining, and complaining in the world around them, thereby experiencing more struggle. Whining and ranting are bloodcurdling signals that it's beyond time to change one's narrative and approach to work.

Most stories of job dissatisfaction are frightening tales of people who unwittingly started down the slippery slope to zombiedom and landed themselves smack dab into the middle of the twilight zone. Although every person's tale is unique, there tend to be some patterns in the narratives that people tell. The following seven types of zombies captures the various narratives. See if any of these sound like you or someone you care about.

1. *Sold Out.* You sold your soul for a paycheck and health benefits. You no longer believe in your company's direction, you don't trust what the leaders are telling you, and you are confused about its vision and mission. Yet your spouse is clinging to the creature comforts you provide and you feel trapped. If you leave your job, you fear you may lose the love in your life or the little luxuries you love to buy—although you would never admit that out loud to anyone. You all might enjoy the things that

the money enables you to buy, but you're questioning if this job is worth the price.

2. *Zombie Boss.* You're giving your all to a job you actually enjoy, but your soul-sucking boss is thwarting you at every turn, taking credit for your work, and intimidating or bullying you or others. You're ready to run to any job at any level just to escape the madness.

3. *Nauseatingly Nostalgic.* You're stuck in the swirl of constant change and the stress-heavy new business world, longing for the good, old days of security and stability. Dreaming of the past, you're disillusioned and disheartened about the future, with no clear path forward.

4. *Zombie Team: Yuck in the Gut.* You can't stand the people you work with and have found yourself on a zombie team. You're not sure how you landed on Planet Whiner, but your team lacks passion, motivation, and innovation. They misuse the company's great benefits and perks systems. Your colleagues are phoning it in daily; a few even hit the bike trail, golf course, or spa when they are supposed to be working, leaving you to hold the bag of accountability. This job is actually making you sick, but you don't see a way to change what you can't stomach.

5. *RIP: Retired in Place.* Your mental countdown to retirement has begun, and you're waiting out the clock to keep your health benefits and save your money a little bit longer. You want to offer your institutional knowledge to the team, but you feel overlooked, irrelevant, and weary.

6. *Runners.* Feel like you were born to run? Find yourself tripping on slower runners as you rush to escape the

dreaded zeds? Running is your means for survival at all costs. No job can meet your high hopes and expectations, as you are wired for disappointment. So you leave company after company looking for a job that challenges you and uses your strengths. You'd rather quit a dozen front-line jobs than find yourself stuck in a rut, but you're starting to run on fumes and that resumé is full of warning signs for potential employers.

7. *Burnt-Out Superhero.* You've always been proud of your efforts and capacity for work. Your boss just compared you to a thoroughbred horse, which you actually thought was a compliment. You have pursued your career and taken care of others for as long as you can recall. Struggling to keep up with family needs, commutes, meals, and extracurricular activities, you have lost sight of what is most meaningful. Absent that motivating spark, you now want to crawl into a corner and take a nap. You run on adrenaline but are too amped up to make needed changes.

Do any of these resonate for you? If so, I want to offer you some hope. You *can* make changes without losing yourself or your career. As Gandhi is often credited with saying, you can "be the change" you wish to experience in your work. If you keep waiting for others to change before you do, you are likely deferring your power, again and again—and that is another surefire way to slip off your own path to fulfillment and zeal.

Yikes, I Might Have Been Infected— How Do I Know for Sure?

Before we delve into how to be the change, let's answer first an important question: Have you become a zombie and/or are you infecting others? The following checklist will help you discover the answer.

Let's face it: You spend most of your time at work, yet you are mentally and emotionally checking out and feeling less and less effective. You owe it to yourself and the people around you to get your groove back. But how do you know how far you've fallen and if you are, indeed, becoming a zombie? Grab a pen or mentally go through the following list, checking off every statement that applies to you.

Zombie Checklist

____I regularly find myself saying, "I don't belong at this job."

____I get out of bed groaning about the day ahead.

____I start dreading Monday on Saturday night.

__I write long e-mails or memos to my boss about ideas I have for meaningful change and never send them. (Why bother?)

__I don't feel heard at work, so I might as well give up trying to speak.

__I'm passed over for leadership roles that should have been mine.

__I regularly wonder if I'll ever achieve anything more than my current position.

__I go out of my way to avoid my coworkers, especially my boss.

__I watch the clock all day, waiting for 5:00 p.m., the time when my real life starts.

__Weekends are made for living, or #WAFL is my weekday mantra!

__I zone out in front of reality TV, living vicariously through others.

__I've sold my soul for a paycheck, and I regret it.

__I'm afraid I'll never have enough, even though I can't define what "enough" is.

__I tell myself I'm happy and engaged, but deep down I know that's not true.

__I'm losing curiosity about the world and the desire to explore the deeper meaning of life and my purpose.

__I'm regularly sucked into workplace gossip and drama, and I often find myself taking sides in "us versus them" conflicts.

__I could be and do so much more, but I don't know where to start.

If you checked five or more of these statements, you're on a slippery slope, but there's still a chance you can dodge the virus. Six to ten? Your family and friends know something's up, even if they can't point to the reason or are afraid to say you are looking a little pale these days. Eleven or more check marks and you're fully zombified, stuck in a dark, damp place on a treadmill to nowhere and possibly scared to take the first step off.

Now that you've completed the Zombie Checklist and you have a clue, don't freak out. As with any change you've made in your life, coming to terms with the idea that change is necessary is the first step. You are clear that change is needed and you are ready to drop the dead skin and go boogie again. That knowing—the clarity about what you don't want to experience any longer—is the key for you to reawaken to purpose and meaning. Let's get going!

Embodied Content

Re– Words: ReAwakening, ReMembering, ReConnecting, ReHumanizing

As you read through the rest of this book, consider and explore the power of *re–*. The section titles "Reawaken," "Remember," "Reconnect," and "Rehumanize" were chosen intentionally to call you back wholeheartedly into your work and to have you reframe your approach and view to play with challenges instead of struggling through them. Each of these words represents an invitation—and a path—back to the light.

1. ReAwaken – an invitation to recognize the voice of your spirit and call it back into your work and life.
2. ReMember – an invitation to remember your unique purpose and significant contribution on this planet, one inspired by the stories of those who have remembered.
3. ReConnect – an invitation to integrate your inner world—head, heart, and will—with your outer world—the people with whom you work every day!
4. ReHumanize – an invitation to shift from an employee-based culture to a spirit-based culture, seeing people not as mere resources to an end, but as humanity—who we are and can become together.

The Latin prefix *re–* means "again and again," or the alpha and the omega. In short, the beginning is the same as the ending. Think about that. The power of *re–* may be the key for acceptance of this notion that *you were always you*, even before you were born into your human body, which simply became your vehicle and means for expression, for living, for connecting, and for contributing. So play with this idea that maybe you were reborn onto this planet to learn and to grow spiritually. Consider how your work was intended to be the playing field for your growth, and you will find the rest of this book—and your life—more interesting.

Reframing this reawakening in this way is both a powerful invocation and a simple reminder to fearlessly move beyond the idea of work as torture. It is an invitation to get jiggy, get moving, and regain a sense of meaning on your path to change—not because you have to, but because you know you can. You were not born to run and hide with workplace zombies: You were born to shine.

ReAwaken

So the message is this:

This is a time for going within.
You may appear to be irresponsible by choosing to do nothing,
Or, by choosing to take a giant leap.
Let it be.
You may struggle trying to change things, situations, or people.
You may find you can only change yourself.
Let it be.
You may want to run back to something familiar when you
glimpse the new.
Acknowledge that desire.
Let it be.
You may feel like your efforts as a leader, a parent, a change agent
go unnoticed.
Let it be.
Love your teams, your children, and your colleagues
wholeheartedly.
Go about the business of personal reflection and *reawaken* to who
you were meant to be.
Then, make the invisible visible. Determine how *visible* you are
willing to be.
Witness the reawakening in others.
And, let it be.
This is all for you to know and to do now.

—DJ Mitsch, Journal entry, July 2005

First Path Back into the Light

ReAwaken

You were born awake to the world, open to so many possibilities, strengths, and gifts. Over the course of a lifetime, important parts of you may have also been stuffed down, snuffed out, or turned dormant through choosing to do what others wanted or through atrophy. That experience may have resulted in your doing work that you were not truly excited about and that led to falling into an unconscious, sleepwalking daze. Think of this part of the book as your runaway alarm clock, rousting you out of that somnambulistic state and waking you to a very powerful part of yourself: your spirit. Why is this important? Waking up to your spirit is the first pathway from zombie to zealot.

Human-Making Kits Require Water and Soul!

Yes, we humans are more than flesh and bones. Sure, your body is made up of a few key ingredients. In fact, 75 percent of it is water. You can buy the other human-making ingredients somewhere in your town between the health food and farm supply stores. Beyond the physical part of your body that can be catalogued in medical textbooks, though, is a part of you that can't be measured by the usual scientific tools. It's your *spirit* (I use the term *soul* interchangeably with *spirit* throughout), which drives you and makes you uniquely you. Working zealots are awake to their spirits and seek guidance from within for their biggest decisions each and every day.

I don't know about you, but I want to work with people who are in touch with their spirits. Those with enough energy to see possibility and hope in any situation have the lights on, challenge greatness, build amazing works of art, share bold ideas, and engage in meaningful conversations. Those qualities come from an intangible place, an aspect of you that is your essence— that intrinsic part of you that makes you, YOU.

I was once asked to present on the topic of "Spirit at Work" to an advanced coaching class at a university. "Spirit is a corporeal intelligence, an energy ingredient in your makeup that is undeniable, allowing you to personally expand or contract efforts and performance depending how you hold, recognize, and integrate it," I explained. That statement inspired a delightful conversation, resulting in the agreement that we are all more than flesh and bones, water and minerals. We remain in a constant state of growth and recreation until we take our last breath. Our spirited conversation continued until we arrived at this agreement: If you are alive, you are a spiritual being. Your spirit is the animating essence of who you are, as much a part of you as your organs.

You can ignore your spirit and lose that vital connection, giving in to the chaos around you. You can deny your spirit or become cynical about it. But by focusing on putting your head down, blending in, or playing small, you're denying your spirit its right to shine, thereby taking the first steps down the zombie path. Like it or not, your spirit is part of you, and recalling it is a critical part of waking up.

Do You Need to Wake Up?

Mind, body, spirit. By now, we've all heard about the mind-body-spirit connection. We know of terms like *work-life balance* too, which point to the idea that as human beings we are more than employees and workers, we are individuals with the need for physical, social, emotional, and spiritual fulfillment too. Most leaders I've coached have no problem understanding the idea that we humans are multidimensional individuals with different facets to our being. They get that our lives have different domains that we can give energy to and that it is possible for imbalances to occur. Figure 2, the Energy Wheel, captures this concept. It contains a circle with categories designed for people to self-assess where they are strong and in good shape and to help them address where they have gaps so they feel more alive and have more energy: contribution, family, mental, spiritual, physical, financial, career, exploration, relationships, and a final category that can be tailored to the specific person. I often use Figure 2 with these leaders to assess the attention they are providing to different life dimensions and to discover areas for growth and rebalancing.

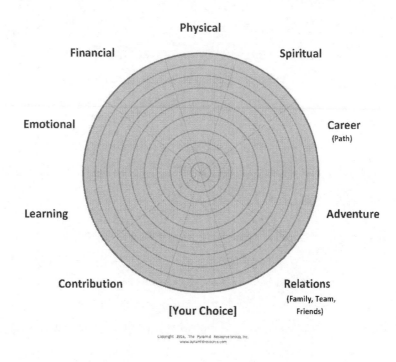

Figure 2. The Energy Balance Wheel

This simple wheel pattern allows a person to take a snapshot of the dimensions that compose a full life and to plot their own degree of attention to each of these areas. It is intended to help determine where a person may want to address a dimension of life that is draining them, while nurturing the areas that are meaningful. (Note: There is a blank Energy Wheel for you to complete in the back of the book in the Zombie Rescue Team Toolkit.) The center is "0" and the outer circle is "10" - or completely attained.

Here's the point. You are not typically a zombie in every area of your life, but if you are a zombie at work, chances are that this condition is affecting other dimensions of your life. It's not hard to imagine how the Burned Out Superhero might end up on the couch watching TV after work, instead of heading to the gym for some exercise or how Yuck in the Gut might avoid after-work happy hour to escape her zombie team even if it means she has no social life. From a positive angle, think of it this way: having a fulfilling and meaningful career shapes how you experience the world, because your trade—your career—is an expression of your spirit, of who you really are and where you spend most of your time. Whatever your career path or daily endeavor, if you are alive at work, chances are you will feel alive outside of work. If you struck with zombiedom at work, chances are that the symptoms carry over to or overshadow some of those really important aspects of your life that are important to you or going well.

Interestingly, when our clients fill out the Energy Wheel, they can readily speak about how they eat and exercise (although many don't talk about vacations or take time for family-first activities). They are eager to share what they are reading and their past education. They can tell you about their families and financial needs—sending their kids to better schools, watching their sports or dances. Some can rattle off facts from the emotional intelligence course they took three years ago to be able to label their feelings. That's a start.

Although many understand what their spirit is—that part of their personality that animates them and holds the rest of their personhood together—most are not clear about what role spirit plays in their workplace performance. Yet possessing strength in all dimensions is critical to playing full out. It is also critical for modeling possibility and leading. Commentators and coaches, when talking about great Olympians or sports heroes, will discuss not only these athletes' physical capabilities but also those intangible characteristics—their drive, their will, their grace—that helped them achieve that higher level of star performance. Businesspeople who value the role that their spirit can play at work open up the possibility of brilliant, inspired performance for themselves and their teams as well.

This idea of reawakening our spirits at work may sound a bit "new age-y" to some, yet it is not a new idea. It is as ancient as mankind. In fact, the philosopher Plato called on his contemporaries many centuries ago to come to life, to reawaken as torchbearers of humanity in this piece of wisdom:

> The souls of people, on their way to Earth-life, pass through a room full of lights; each takes a taper—often only a spark—to guide it in the dim country of this world. But some souls, by rare fortune, are detained longer—and have time to grab a handful of tapers, which they weave into a torch. These are the torchbearers of humanity—its poets, seers, and saints, who lead and lift the race out of darkness, toward the light. They are the law-givers and saviors, the light-bringers, way-showers and truth-tellers, and without them, humanity would lose its way in the dark.
>
> —Plato

Pick up Your Torch

Plato was right.

Humanity needs torchbearers now like never before, before we all lose our way and fall prey to the zombie outbreak. Today's torchbearers aren't just poets and saints. They're great team leaders, teachers, coaches, technology natives, innovators, problem solvers, psychologists, and executives. They are the souls who care deeply about humanity. I like the idea of calling leaders *light workers*. Isn't that the real role of those whose primary responsibility is to illuminate the best in others? We can all be light workers and way showers of humanity if we take the time to simply ignite and tend our own inner flame. If we do that, we give other people around us complete permission to do the same. They can warm up in the glow and defrost their frozen parts. And this is what they will say about you when you are awake and ignited, "I always felt better when I was in her/his company. S/ He changed my life!"

If this message of zeal, passion, light, and positive change speaks to you as a leader, a coach, a parent, or anyone who cares deeply about your fellow people, then there is hope for us all. You can transform yourself and others from zombies to zealots. This is y/our time, y/our chance, to become who you were meant to be and to contribute your best to the expanding universe! We need you.

I've worked with medicine men and women over the years who teach rituals. One of those, "calling your spirit back," is used when people have suffered and their spirits are wounded or have left the body behind for some reason. When I began writing this,

I also found a story attributed to unnamed elders of the Hopi Nation,[3] that points out a simple but urgent truth: *We are the ones we have been waiting for.* This excerpt resonates on so many levels with my message:

> Gather yourselves!
>
> Banish the word "struggle" from your attitude and your vocabulary.
>
> All that you do now must be done in a sacred manner - and in celebration.
>
> *"We are the ones we have been waiting for."*

Stop Struggling!

Let me put this point forward quite simply: Stop struggling. Stop freaking out about anything that has to do with myths in your life. Remember that the things you worry about—the stories that you make up—are usually something that got stuck in your amygdala and are just not true. Stop worrying about how your life is turning out so far or if you are enough. YOU are! Start right here, right now, to make the changes you seek. This one simple shift is a surefire way to get beyond the feeling of "work as too much effort" or the pitfall of buying into zombie tales that you "can't do something because [insert your excuse here]."

I hear the word *struggle* in most stories people tell about challenges in their workplace culture, even if the cultures are proclaimed to be people-centric and pretty cool. People are conditioned to whine about "us versus them" until they awaken to understand that "they's us and we's them." That means that whatever you are judging to be annoying or disturbingly true about other people is also true for you at some level and is obvious to others, even if you can't see it in yourself. Think you have a zombie team? They may think you are the Zombie Boss or team mate. One of the first perspectives we coaches offer is to shift people away from complaining or ranting—a key behavior on the slippery slope to becoming a zombie—by calling it out and stating the obvious, such as "It sounds like you feel victimized here. That's no fun. What would happen if you made some bold requests instead of complaining about this situation? Behind every complaint is a request you haven't made of someone who can do something about it. What are those requests?"

Catch the word *struggle* and shift it to the word *play*. A statement like "I'm struggling with how to go about this new way of leading" becomes "I'm playing with how to go about this new way of leading." That simple change in the language changes the collective narrative, illuminating new possibilities.

Warning: Reawakening May Make You Miserable Enough to Run and Hide *at First!*

Reawakening to our spirit can unsettle us. It often demands we change direction and take bold action. Many of us are content with the status quo, even if it means being complacent with misery. You might hate your job, but the idea of leaving it to find work that feeds your soul can be terrifying, especially if the work you want is completely different from the work you're currently doing.

We might remember moments of joy in our past when we felt most alive and present—an art class, a school play, a creative writing workshop, a surfing lesson—but deny ourselves today any possibility other than the life we're living. We tell ourselves we won't make enough money, we have too many responsibilities, and happiness and fulfillment are for other people. So we give up and stay the course instead of risking change. We never consider creating space for something new and investing time in our imaginations or big ideas. We give in to the zombie mind-set without realizing that our spirits are right there waiting to help us create something amazing. These invisible aspects of us are always awake, waiting to create, be engaged, or be freed. As Lao Tzu said,

> At the center of your being
> you have the answer:
> you know who you are
> and you know what you want.

Take a moment to play with this: Close your eyes. Think of the word *reawaken*. What images does it bring to mind for you? What kinds of emotions and feelings does it stir up? Are you angry that you haven't done what you set out to do? Do you constantly ruminate over the big question, "What am I going to do with my life?"

If so, know you have company. One reason I find people constantly asking themselves these types of questions is because of the way they have been packaged and reviewed as workers. People get stuck in positions, and that static state feeds into narratives of disempowerment in which their lives do not meet their or someone else's expectations.

You are so much more than a title or position. Have you considered lately that you are more for your company than any of the following? (Circle those that you've heard.)

Table 1

The Employee Label Table

BTHs (Bless Their Hearts)	Bottom 10 Percent	Boss
Clock Watchers	Contractors	Crew
Direct Reports	Diverse Candidates	Double Dipper(Retired/ Rehired)
Drivers	Exempt Employees	Emos
Extroverts	Fast Trackers	FTEs (Full-Time)
Geeks	Hands (as in Hired Hands)	Head Count
Heavy Hitters	High Performers	HiPos (High Potentials)
Human Capital	Human Resources	Introverts
Integrated Talent	Lifers	Key Contributors
Living Dead	Low Man on the Totem Pole	Maintenance
Micromanagers	Movers and Shakers	New Dogs
Newbies	Nonexempt Employees	Old Dogs
Old-Timers	Paper Chasers/Pushers	Part-Timers
Placeholders	Production Line	Project Managers
Propeller Heads	Redheaded Stepchildren	Replacements
Resources	RIP (Retired in Place)	Salaried
Short Timers	Show Dogs	Slackers and Doers
Sole Contributors	Staff	Steady Eddies
Subordinates	Superiors	Talent Managers
Tightwads	Top Guns	Top Talent
Top 20 Percent	Troopers	Knuckle-Draggers
Wannabes	Workers	Zombies

The thing about Labels

Our team cataloged some of the names we've heard over the years used to define or categorize people, as can be seen in Table 1. While these labels may provide a short-hand inside organizations, this raises a couple of questions for us:

What do "they" call you? (Anything on this list?)
What do you want to be called?

Are you a mover and shaker? A tyrant? The low man on the totem pole? The top 10%? What do you want to be known for? What would you like for others to call you?

You are more than any position you hold, any role you play, or any box you serve to check in your organization. And who you are—your essence, the part of you that is indelible and lives on—is worthy of full expression. Maybe you and those who lead and manage you need to be reminded of that.

The Practice of Calling Your Spirit Back

Aboriginal peoples, religious leaders from every discipline around the world, and modern mystics share ancient rituals and common truths. Do unto others as you would have them do unto you—otherwise known as the Golden Rule—is a tenet of cultures around the world. This is the invitation to notice that whatever energy we put out in the world will be returned to us in our experiences. Thoughts are focused energy and very powerful. We can consciously choose them, instead of having them run amok with fear the way they do when we are living and working on autopilot, unconsciously in motion. Choosing life and new perspective is how we create our future and how we learn to really see and experience more fully the world around us.

Gandhi said it this way:

> Your beliefs become your thoughts,
> Your thoughts become your words,
> Your words become your actions,
> Your actions become your habits,
> Your habits become your values,
> Your values become your destiny.

Like attracts like is a simple law of physics. The good news is that the more energy and vitality we exude, the easier it becomes to share it and have it returned. Sending out goodwill and positivity connects you to your essence, your spirit's most natural state. The bad news? Negativity—numbing out—attracts more of that into your experiences too. Knuckle dragging begets more knuckle draggers.

Your significant contribution to the game of life begins when you recognize that your happiness is paramount to connecting you with the life of your dreams. Working on that attainment is your birthright and likely why you are in the game of life on this planet. Likewise, your unhappiness, anger, disappointment, shame, or even rage disconnects you from experiencing the life you desire and keeps you disconnected. It's time to call on your own spirit to hop, jump, or walk back into a body that is ready to stand in your own power and experience life more fully.

Six Ways to Reawaken Your Spirit

You can reawaken your spirit by literally calling *It* back
to you in any number of ways. I have found that many of
my clients like the idea of daily rituals to get in touch with
their inner spark. Here are a few to get you started.

1. Wake up and set an intention for your day. Breathe
    deeply and seal the feeling of this experience in
    your heart space; breathe deeply again to seal that
    experience or feeling in your gut. Next, set a positive
    intention; imagine your best day, mentally walking
    through your office, store, or school. Call to your
    mind's eye those experiences you most desire. Then
    hit the floor dancing as if it has already happened.
    (It's a matter of metaphysics: The universe fills the
    void between you and what you have imagined.)
    If you are a healthy human being, but get stuck in
    fearful and miserable patterns it seems to make more
    of that struggle available to you. If you genuinely
    appreciate all the gifts you have, the things that are
    working, it gives you more of that.
2. When you are brushing your teeth, tell yourself
    that you are amazing. A sudsy smile is a great way
    to start the day!
3. Keep a gratitude journal. Believe it or not, there
    is an app for that! You can start by being grateful

for something small, such as ice cream or a good night's sleep. Then notice the texture and quality this exercise takes. A change agent friend of mine keeps a word a day in his mobile app of things he feels grateful for. The week of Thanksgiving, he publishes the list. It includes things like "grits, traffic lights, pickles, sheet cake, kid laughter, Petticoat Junction" (or other old TV reruns that make him laugh). Entries consist of just one or two words each, but what dividends those words pay! When I get the message, I read it twice over. It brings me back to the state of awe that we are amazing creatures and that we are surrounded by beauty. It has become one of my favorite treats at Thanksgiving.

4. Play music. Music is your life's sound track. Certain songs remind you of places you've been—play those that remind of you of happy times. Music feeds the soul and keeps our stories alive, taking us to places we've been or long to be, giving us themes, lifting our spirits. A wise healer once said to me, "Music is how the universe works through cosmic problems. The masters of music write an opus or a symphony unconsciously solving a universal riddle." Go listen to some classical music by the masters and see if you can determine what riddle was solved.

5. Stretch behind your desk. Sit on a yoga ball, walk, or use the stairs instead of the elevator. Take a few

deeps breaths and really notice the people around you before you get into your car or catch that train or plane. Take time at least twice a day to stand up, bend over, and touch your toes. Lack of flexibility in your body is a sign that you lack flexibility in other parts of your life. If you can touch the floor or your toes, celebrate and put that in your gratitude journal! If you can't, get moving!

6. Get in touch with your spirit. While you can't really tickle yourself—seriously, try it—you can jump-start your day by connecting with the still small voice of your spirit and higher consciousness – recognizing YOUR voice of wisdom is your best guide. Declare who you really are and what you most want to manifest and experience - "I am amazing and worthy good things. I am ready to hear, see, appreciate, understand, learn from, or accept guidance to work in new ways. I am at my best today and it's my turn to shine!"

Your spirit is a complex thing for any writer or even the world's most noteworthy gurus to describe. It is embodied within you and it is somewhere beyond you. It is an energetic essence that connects you to every life form and everyone else—the good and the not so good. It shows up in your body as your intuition, your gut, your instincts, and always as your wisdom. It has kept you safe from harm and it has always been there awaiting your recognition, although we humans have had it processed out of us for generations. So reclaim it now and tune in to see what can really happen next.

The "What If" Game

It can help to take on a fresh perspective. When we become parents, we see things with new (although sometimes sleepy) eyes. When my children were born, I immediately saw in them a wisdom that was ancient. As I rocked them to sleep, I was struck by a conviction that before they learn language, children are completely connected to all realms or dimensions of reality. They are truly tapped into their spirit and connected to the spaces and faces around them.

I'm convinced that children who are being born now are here on a mission to save the planet. I believe they are here to shepherd in new consciousness. Millennial children and Generation X, Y, Z kids are technology natives who have quickly accelerated the communication game, connecting us all. If you look up and out, you, too, will realize that they are more than your babies: They are here with other profound gifts we need to honor as well. I trust that we will all benefit from the energy they bring, even if they rock our world at first and even if we don't like or fully understand their methods. My point is to see them this way and nurture them so that their truest nature takes root.

So what does the wisdom of babies have to do with zombies, zealots, workplace shifts, and fresh perspectives? Babies are full of wonder, able to see things in a new way, and always learning. That wonder, that ability to see with new eyes, can be a gift to someone who has lost his or her sight and way and has inadvertently slipped off the path.

Let's play a "what if" game to create a new perspective about fuller ownership of our lives and careers.

What if . . .

- ❖ we really are born here on Earth to play an extraordinary game called Life?
- ❖ our workplaces are actually the playing field for our soul's evolution?
- ❖ you knew at birth everything there was to know about your life blueprint and what you were meant to be and do?
- ❖ we choose our parents and the situation we are born into as part of how we enter the game?
- ❖ you are completely connected to all of creation and know how to use the laws of nature to attract all of the resources you will ever need?
- ❖ soul mates from other lives have agreed to challenge us during this lifetime and show up as that zombie boss, that SOB partner, that difficult spouse, that renegade kid?
- ❖ we sign up for our gifts and talents and come into the world knowing how we will use them and the events that catalyze how we discover them?
- ❖ we took full ownership of, well, everything?
- ❖ we recognized that forgiveness is a path to evolving and becoming our most powerful self?

So many people are disconnected from their values; the way they'd love to operate; and being honest, real, and authentic: all the things people want to be and claim to be when they're at their best. So many forces in your life might be demanding that dishonesty from you: the shareholders in your organization, the higher-ups, the pieces of your company that are outside the realm of daily operations. Truly living your values—playing the game according to your rules—can set you free and wake you up. It can also be the invitation and model for others to follow.

That level of ownership in your life will give you insights and a sense of control. You can take the field each day knowing that you're in charge of the game instead of focusing on what isn't working. Seeing yourself as the key player in your own game of life will push you to embrace challenges as opportunities. Your experiences at work are just plays in the game. You decide the outcome.

What if you were so powerful that you could manifest anything you imagined?

You already are that powerful and, in fact, you already do create all that you imagine. So start imagining great things!

Reawaken! Realize that no matter what your age, whether you are twenty-two or sixty-five, now is the time to unleash your best on the world around you!

A friend said this to me when were trained as trainers on an outdoor ropes courses together. She quoted Napoleon Hill just as we were about to do the sky walk above the ground on a tightrope: "Whatever your mind can conceive and believe the mind can achieve."[4] I imagined I could do that tightrope thing with ease. And I did, until I asked for help and was misunderstood, which I interpreted as "ignored." At that point, I gave up on the activity and came down on belay, not realizing how close I was to the goal of hitting the crow's nest and riding the zip line through the woods. So I had to start over, learning to believe and stay with it until I achieved my fun goal to zip through a forest at 70 miles per hour.

What do you believe about who you are?

Is that belief the first thing that needs to change?

Being told that something is "all in your mind" is often seen as dismissive and judgmental. Yet changing your thinking—how you hold and process those ideas that get caught in your brain—is critical when it comes to making positive changes in your life and work. It's also good to know that you have the important tools in hand (and in your head) already, so expand the power tool of choice. We always have a series of choices, and selecting our emotions and our thoughts is a little like shopping for clothes. The more we try on, the more we understand what fits best. You know why zombies are always searching for brains? Because your brain holds your creativity and can animate your muscles and mind to protect you. It is your learning center. It helps you process all the things that happen. It allows you to consciously choose how you respond to the world with the "feelings" of love and gratitude when you are "feeling" most afraid and stuck.

Reawakening as a first step to reclaiming your on-the-job happiness involves jump-starting your thought processes so that you are able to see your situation differently. It involves taking inventory of your qualities and values and consciously calling out to your spirit to serve as a guide and inspiration for your future progress. All of these things might have slipped from your consciousness while you were in a zombie state, but once you bring them back to mind and remember who *you* are, you'll be ready to start analyzing your situation and figuring out what you can do about it.

ReMember

You are who you are
You are not what you do
You are not what others say about you,
not the labels in your company,
not the labels from family or friends.
You may play many roles in your world, but you
are more than the sum of these
ReMember
Not just who you wanted to be
Remember
You become who you really are when you understand your contribution.
Now go. Become. Work at something that
Is meaningful and demands the best in you!
Lead yourself and others.
You be YOU!

DJ's Manuscript Journal, October 2015

Second Path Back into the Light

ReMember

Reawakening is about consciousness. With an awakened spirit, you are ready to remember who you really are. What is your purpose on this planet? Where do you want to play most fully? If you were in touch with the most authentic you—strengths, passions, interests, preferences—where would you contribute or play your best role now?

There is a path of remembering for each of us: remembering what excites us, what moves us, and what drives us forward to keep living and engaging. Remembering that we have choices about how we spend our time and where we invest our energy. Remembering that we don't have to follow others' expectations for us or someone else's script. We are here to be us and no one else. You are you and I am me and she is she; together we make a kaleidoscope of society that ensures we all have what we need: inventors, revolutionary thinkers, doctors, lawyers, teachers, business people, bus drivers, bread bakers, and brilliant spirits in every corner of our world.

We all take a journey on the path of remembering—the path of consciousness—at some point in our lives, although many step away from the personal power they experience along the way. Most people find the truth of their own brilliance and potential to be quite scary. That fear can cause people to choose limiting or small games as they cling to safer routes for their careers and life choices.

Marianne Williamson wrote a memorable essay on the topic of fear that Nelson Mandela quoted in his inauguration and many have attributed to him.[5] It starts with these three lines:

> Our deepest fear is not that we are inadequate.
> Our deepest fear is that we are powerful beyond measure.
> It is our light, not our darkness, that we are most afraid of.

That statement was a life-changing quote for me. I understand it and I have lived it; I think that it can be said of most people who spend a lifetime exploring their inner realm. It is also true for so many who are hiding out now, perhaps even you.

What would happen if we found the courage to let go of the fear and replaced it with belief in possibility? What would happen if we saw all of the choices before us and selected the ones that were just right for us? I am reminded of the following lines from one of my past, undated journal entries:

> *"Life is a banquet, but most poor suckers starve to death staring at the bounty. And sometimes it is WE who are consumed by the world as its most delicious main course."*

In a July 2005 journal entry, I continued on the same point: "There are days I am sure I am dining at a banquet of abundance—so many opportunities, resources, and love in my life. And there are days I stare into space, frozen in my ability to make a clear choice about what I most want to be or do next. It is often easier to just stop as if I were waiting for someone to escort me back to a familiar place. There are so many options in front of us if we will simply open our eyes to behold them. Each day I come to a choice point just like all others—I choose to remember who I really am and act out of alignment with that—I work for the highest good—or I become a main meal for the blood suckers I give my power to.

Thoughts from my Journal entry, July 2005

As I reviewed my journal in prep for writing this book, I read these entries a few times. The notion that people starve to death looking at life's bounty is descriptive. We've become so much a part of the consumer, comparative, paradoxical world that we forget we are divinely designed and powerfully creative. The buffet of life awaits us and it is up to us to pick and choose the meal we want to eat. Remembering who you are—what calls you and fills you—is the path to the light.

This section of the book is filled with stories about people who called themselves more fully into their work after remembering who they were and are, setting themselves up for more exciting and fulfilling lives. The stories are written to illustrate each of the seven Zombie to Zealot archetypes described in the beginning of the book.

Seven Case Studies:
Zombified People Come Back to Life!

In the introduction, I briefly discussed the seven most common types of zombies that high achievers morph into in the workplace. The seven illustrations and brief stories that follow illustrate the experiences of amazing and talented people just like you who found themselves on a slippery slope to becoming zombies by forgetting that they had options and a buffet of opportunities laid out before them. They temporarily lost their place in line on their own life's adventure as they gave way to others' power and forgot that they choose their vocation, their career, their job, their company, and their location. The people I feature on the following pages took solid actions to remember their purpose and came back to life in their work, even though, just like you, they found themselves staring into space at some point, too.

Note that these are pseudo names, morphed stories and representative samples of heroes we've coached. No one is identified or exposed unless I had expressed written permission to fearlessly share their story. The point in sharing these stories is to notice the patterns and check in to see if you relate, as there are so many people in each of these categories based on our experiences.

1. Sold Out

The Bones: Sold my soul for paycheck. Lifestyle costs mounting. Still owe $250K for my MBA. No financial freedom to move or change careers. Kids cost a million dollars a year. Dreams on the back burner. I take care of everyone else first. Not even sure what I truly love to do. I hate Mondays.

The Skinny: Mary typed out a furious e-mail to her new supervisor and hit *send* without editing it. The supervisor had asked her ten minutes before day's end to compile a thirty-page budget report for the supervisor to review over the weekend, on top of Mary's already demanding list of tasks that she needed to finish, which was long enough to keep three Marys busy. Although Mary loved the nature of her work, she simply had too much to do. She felt trapped in her role at a fast-growing international company, where layers of new team members were constantly being added as direct reports and cutbacks elsewhere left Mary with more and more work.

Seven years ago, Mary had been aggressively recruited. She'd leveraged her way to a high six-figure salary with annual bonuses. She'd felt in control and recruited a stellar team. Now she was increasingly unsure that she could perform in a way that would meet her supervisor's and her company's unrealistic expectations.

From the outside, Mary's life was perfect. She had a company car and a beautiful home on a nearby lake. Her three kids were in private school and her husband moonlighted as a chef in a gourmet restaurant on the weekends, providing childcare during the week. Others depended on her, from her aging parents who'd given her power of attorney over their affairs to her friends who relied on her to organize monthly birthday outings and activities. Underneath the perfect veneer, Mary was overwhelmed, longing for recognition, and desperate to feel as though her work really mattered.

As soon as she hit *send* on the e-mail to her supervisor, the color drained from Mary's face. *What was I thinking?* she berated herself. *Couldn't I have taken a minute to edit my response?* She knew in that moment she was overwhelmed, exhausted from taking care of everyone else and having her every action questioned at work. She needed her job—but at what cost? And if she found the courage to walk away, how could she possibly start over and maintain her current salary and lifestyle?

The Heart: Mary came to me for coaching after her disastrous e-mail. I asked her, "What do you really want to be doing?" Mary told me she'd been a second chair violinist in high school and college. During those years, she attended summer music camps at Julliard. She longed to dust off her violin, which had been a gift from her grandfather, and play again, but she never found the time. "What's the fear?" I asked. Mary explained that her husband enjoyed his life and that her kids' schools were expensive; she didn't want to let them down by walking away from her job. Mary enjoyed the benefits of her salary, too, and she wasn't ready to quit. Walking away wasn't an option at the moment; it was time to resolve the crisis she'd created at work.

The No-Brainer: Instant reaction to stimuli is the most typical style of communication in any organization. "WTF?" is often our first response when we're overwhelmed, incredulous, or frustrated. Heated and defensive responses can make a bad situation worse. In the absence of real dialogue, people have limited room for interpretation, and misunderstandings amplify.

Mary and I worked out an approach. She made her way to her new supervisor's office and said, "I owe you an apology. I overreacted to your request the other afternoon, and I would like to have a conversation about why and what we can do to set a new course for our work together."

The conversation that followed paved the way to a new understanding between Mary and her supervisor. Mary apologized for her reaction, indicating, "I know I can be intense and that I can overreact. I will work on being more responsive and test my assumptions instead." Her supervisor revealed that she had asked so much of Mary because Mary's institutional knowledge was invaluable in helping her learn the ropes of the job and company, both of which were new to her. She also needed help training up the next level of employees, who were intended to be the cavalry charging in to take some of the pressure and work off of Mary's shoulders. The talk, which flowed naturally and in a nonconfrontational way, allowed her to find common ground with her supervisor and made her realize how much she was respected within her company. Once both women had a handle on a new level of communication, it was easy to discuss a new way forward.

Mary realigned her duties and became a mentor to the new, younger generation of leaders in her organization. Mary did something important outside of work, too: She signed up for weekly violin lessons to refresh her skills and began playing violin a few times a week. Her practices sessions were short, but they gave Mary renewed patience and energy for the regular challenges she faced in the workplace.

Have the Guts: The next time you find yourself in Mary's position, ready to shoot off a response in anger, take a minute to think through the events leading up to the situation. Where are you stopping short of communicating fully with others who need to understand and work with you? If you work on communicating in an effective fashion, like taking the time to step into someone's office or arranging an in-person meeting, you may be able to prevent damaging communication in the heat of the moment, like a misfired e-mail, and get the results you want instead.

Consider, too, those conversations that leave you feeling victimized. Shift your thinking from "WTF?" to "What's the fear?" Once you ask yourself this question, notice how long you continue to defend your need to be right and protect yourself. What fear is driving your reaction? What hidden desires are festering?

The Path Back to Zealing Out: Zealing out starts when you create space in your life by speaking the truth, especially to yourself, about what you most want right now. What is true for you that you haven't voiced? Are you afraid that you will lose status, family respect, peer respect, or love if you take a different path to honor your gifts? Can you imagine making your heart's desire an avocation that might become your vocation someday in the near future? If you refused to sell out for a paycheck, what new decisions and behaviors might you engage in?

Make a game of meeting others' knee-jerk reactions with curiosity. Whenever someone exclaims "WTF?" in your presence, ask the question, "What's the fear?" Stay with the dialogue until you can find common ground. Think, too, about prompting some shifts in perspective and water cooler conversations with the simple shout-out, "WTF? Where's the fun?"

2. Zombie Boss

The Bones: I say *yes* when I mean *no*, I am the new *yes* man. Can't score a transfer. Looking for a hero or deus ex machina to get me out of this place. The heck with seniority, surely a recruiter has something better for me. Not brave enough to speak my truth to those in power. My boss is dismissive and intimidating to me. He is a bully and his very presence zombifies us.

The Skinny: Sandra had been in a leadership role for many years and had an excellent working relationship with her boss. He provided regular input and direction to Sandra for their team without micromanaging her; he also supported Sandra's decisions as if she were an extension of himself. In turn, when he traveled, Sandra had the skills and confidence to lead the team. She was able to handle the day-to-day realignments with the shared vision and team activities, and her team worked seamlessly regardless of whether Sandra's boss was in or out of the office. When Sandra's boss retired and was replaced with someone new, the daily approach to work, trust, and respect that Sandra had enjoyed with her former boss dissolved.

Sandra's new boss felt he needed to establish authority—and he did it by demoting Sandra without discussion. "How could this happen?" she asked herself. "What did I do wrong? Why doesn't he know what I can do?" After years of career growth, Sandra had gone backward in both position and compensation and she felt invisible. As time went on, things with her boss didn't improve. She missed out on several opportunities for advancement when her boss wouldn't rewrite her job description or even let her know positions in her area of expertise were available for pursuit. Sandra knew she wasn't happy, but she wasn't sure what to do next.

The Heart: Sandra was unable to make inroads with her zombie boss. After searching her heart, Sandra decided to make a move that was extraordinarily bold for someone who had been loyal to her boss at all costs: She sought other opportunities in her company by requesting a list of internal postings from her organization's human resources representative. Her inner voice of wisdom compelled her to take a chance. She interviewed with a division president who was forming a new role in the company. After acing the interview, she was offered and accepted a new role for forming a business excellence team—something outside of her experience. It was scary to move out of a position she had mastered, but the joy of escaping her zombie boss reenergized her. In her new role, with her as the new leader, she was able to speak clearly about what lessons she had learned from recent experiences and about what she felt was needed to build trust in the larger organization. Her messages and the level of ownership she demonstrated resonated with the executive vice president of the division. Sandra was able to feel valued again when she leveraged what she had learned in her old positions to build new programs.

The No-Brainer: Sandra paid attention to how the game was unfolding and trusted her intuition. Her heart was telling her it was time to move on because her current boss had created a toxic environment and it was no longer a healthy place for her to work. She also trusted that the years of experience and her commitment to the company would serve her well as she interviewed internally for a new, high-impact position. Sometimes we have to take what we have mastered in one area and share it in another. The most difficult step of the process is making that leap of faith.

Have the Guts: Courage is demonstrated when you find your will, your inner strength to do and say what you have always feared doing or saying. Zombies are cowards. Zealots are bold truth tellers. Sandra had the courage to take action instead of giving up hope and waiting for the next series of changes.

The Path Back to Zealing Out:

A Formula for Truth-Telling

Truth-telling is simple but not easy. Try this truth-telling formula, which I represent with the acronym AIR:

1. Action or behavior that you want to address
2. Impact that it is having on you specifically
3. Request for change

Use this formula to tell yourself the truth first, then share what you feel and think with the person who can hear it and do something about it, especially the boss. It might sound like this:

"I am afraid to say this, but I really need to let you know [the truth to be told]."

"The impact on me and others is this."

"It's time for me to move on and I am looking for another role that feeds my spirit."

Then be ready to take the action to do so.

3. Nauseatingly Nostalgic

The Bones: This place used to be great. I've been here since the beginning and don't recognize it anymore. I change job titles like other people change shoes. Stock options don't give me a say in how this place is run. I'd like no change for a change. It's hard to feel safe when every day's another earthquake. Ah, the good old days. Reminiscing keeps me going. Every time I get up to speed, something changes and I have to start all over: Why bother? Coworkers are jumping ship. Auto response: "I can't."

The Skinny: Jim spent thirty years working for "his" company, one he helped build in a field that he loved. Then the company was purchased by a multinational holding company. The good news was that Jim did well with his stock options. The bad news was that everything changed. Instead of continuing to nurture the gratifying long-term client relationships Jim and his partners had grown, the new management wanted the seasoned players to find small businesses to purchase. Jim found himself in one turnaround project after another. Acquisitions mounted and profit margins dropped. He was called out in every all-hands meeting for not meeting the new company goals. Jim was going through the motions, and his heart was not in the game. He was running on fumes.

The Heart: In the midst of Jim's work frustrations, a close friend and colleague had a heart attack and died suddenly. He was the same age as Jim, and their kids had grown up together. Jim's friend's death was a wake-up call; he was terrified. Could the same thing happen to him? At the same time, Jim's company was pressuring him to take on more work. He was overwhelmed and couldn't sleep. He fell into a deep depression, and his wife threatened to leave him.

The No-Brainer: Realizing that he was at a crisis point, Jim felt moved to move. He deliberately made his life his next turnaround project and got going with vigor. He hired a coach, took his wife's advice to work on their communication through therapy, and dusted off a longtime goal to pursue his doctorate. He had once loved his job, but with the corporate culture having so drastically changed, it was time for him to move on. Jim and his wife sold their monster house, took their kids out of private schools, and relocated to a university town where Jim could teach in an executive MBA program while he completed his doctorate coursework. His kids were fully on board with Project: Reignite Dad because they could see how excited Jim was to make this change. His wife became part of his personal support team, too, participating in all major decisions that affected the family. Surprisingly, it only took three months to make his plans, sell the house, pack for the move, and get to the point where he could walk out the door of a company he had helped to build without feeling like he'd left any loose ends. Once Jim became clear on what he wanted, he was able to let go of the past and his nostalgia for the good old days. Things move fast when we humans clarify our intentions; the creative, problem-solving part of our brains activate and help us to galvanize change.

Jim's employees threw him a going-away party and thanked him profusely for all he had contributed over the years to their development. They also gave him a standing ovation when he detailed the process of his decision making and expressed how happy he was to be going back to school.

Have the Guts: Shifting from frozen to ignited—remembering what it is that drives you—requires that you begin to see where you have been stuck. Becoming exuberant may require dramatic changes in your life plan, including where you live, what you do, how you express yourself, and how you connect with family and others. You may have to first identify the things that don't give you any joy and start deleting them. Give yourself permission to dream and you will soon know what you want to add to your life. Find your courage and go for it!

The Path Back to Zealing Out: Finding your zeal requires that you answer some soul-searching questions:

1. Is this position worth the personal costs to you and your family?
2. Have things changed so much at the office that you feel stuck, frozen, or unable to find a way out?
3. Are you waiting for someone else to ignite you or give you a reason to change?

If you feel like you are running in place, ask a stretch-goal question and generate a new conversation with that little committee that lives in your head—you know, all those archetypal voices that repeat back to you messages from your past, like "Don't do that, you won't make enough money!" and "How will you earn a living doing THAT?"

Instead, ask yourself the following questions:

1. What if this is the most exciting place anyone could ever hope to work?
2. What if this is the place to achieve my personal vision? What if it isn't?
3. What can I do to change the business? Who can I talk to about what is needed?
4. What's the first step now to make my career and future a happier place to land?
5. If my own life is my next project plan, what changes would I make to reignite myself in a way that feeds my spirit and serves others?

4. Zombie Team: Yuck in the Gut

The Bones: I can't stand my coworkers. They live on cheese and whine and act like they're always hung over. No competent help. I'll do what I can, but fixing what's broken is above my pay grade. Thank heaven for sick days. Does the local fast-food joint need counter help?

The Skinny: Mo was all too familiar with the need to belong or fit in. He was one of seven children and the first generation in his family to live in the United States. He had traveled every continent with his family by the time he was twenty years old, which had taught him how to accept differences among people. Mo had little tolerance for people who were intolerant. Then he took a job at a small manufacturing company in the deep southern United States, where the organizational culture was one of intolerance unless you came from near there. Individuals would mass e-mail discriminatory jokes, and team meetings were marked by inflexibility and cultural insensitivity. To cope, Mo developed an argumentative style. He debated any colleague who displayed intolerance and insensitivity and made sure he always had the last word. This approach was exhausting, though, and Mo dreaded driving to work each day. "Every day I wake up with yuck in my gut," he told his father. He spent less than a year at that job before he had to escape the environment.

Mo left his job for a new role in a small, fast-growing tech company as a project manager. His team comprised several people who, like him, had grown up as global citizens, as well as four other people who had lived in southern states all their lives. Whereas Mo got along fine with his more worldly coworkers, he found himself feeling yuck in the gut all over again when he was around his four other coworkers. When one of them asked Mo a question or tried to explain to him how certain things were traditionally done in the office, Mo perceived this as a sign that they were intolerant of him. Mo unconsciously projected his past experiences onto his new coworkers, creating a contentious barrier to protect himself from experiencing more gut "yuck."

The new team leader hired a coach from my company to accelerate the team's development. As the team came together to form their game plan, Mo found himself called out for his negative attitude and constant second-guessing of team leadership. Turns out some of these folks had "yuck in the gut" about working with Mo. Finally, the coach met privately with Mo. "I know you've had unpleasant experiences in the past," she told him. "I challenge you to give your new team a chance and to come to work thinking you will enjoy being here with each of them. It's time to shift your perspective from debate to engagement." Mo needed to up his game and reposition himself as an influencer and a collaborator.

The Heart: Over the course of the four-month team coaching experience, Mo warmed up to the shift from being the King of Muck, who made waves so that everyone shared his yuck-in-the-gut seasickness, to Ship's Captain, who brought his crew together to achieve big things, soon after his one-on-one session with the coach. Mo decided to take a chance and try to engage people in the spirit of possibility and creation. It worked. He discovered that his four coworkers weren't intolerant after all; his ability to work with them, and vice versa, really took off. As the team celebrated project completion, Mo was rewarded with a most valuable teammate plaque and celebrated new friendships.

The No-Brainer: Mo had wanted to believe that people were fair and just. He had believed he would be able to fit in anywhere in the world. He hadn't been prepared for the discrimination he faced in his first job. Debating, challenging, and grumbling until his colleagues either submitted to or dismissed him had become a pattern for Mo. He'd given up on the idea of collaboration and engagement with others. And he wasn't "having any fun, which meant no one else should either!"

Have the Guts: Many leaders and individuals just like you get that yucky feeling when they are in constant swirls of gossip and change. They can encounter the yuck-in-the-gut sensation about their colleagues and respond by challenging the status quo and finding their voice as the loud and sole dissenter. Digging in, being stubborn and right, or debating can be effective in the short term, but it costs you a lot of emotional and mental energy. Sound familiar? To shift from King of Muck to Ship's Captain requires first that you see the potential in others—their light. Set aside your own negative beliefs for a moment and try to imagine the best version of someone you work with. Even if he or she doesn't act that way every day, that person is still capable of such goodness. Your vision of that person's best self is your glimpse of their inner light.

The Path Back to Zealing Out: Zealing out is contagious. Once Mo transitioned from debating to dialogue, he was able to become a positive contagion in his office rather than a source of negativity and strain. His method of problem solving became to simply approach others in a state of inquiry, allowing them to feel comfortable sharing their ideas. Collaboration followed. You, too, can turn a solo stand-up act into a dialogue. Choose inquiry over debate. And when you find yourself feeling yuck in the gut regarding a colleague, ask yourself, "What can I learn from this person, right now? How can I see the best in him or her and acknowledge his or her light?"

5. RIP: Retired in Place

The Bones: I'm just counting the days until retirement. In it for the benefits. No need to evolve or change. Must be doing something right: The paychecks still cash. Holding on for the next buyout. Retirement countdown app on my smartphone. I know everything about this place, not that the institutional knowledge helps me now. No one asks. Weary—just trudging through.

The Skinny: Walter had been in the crop science business for decades. Raised on a farm in the Midwest, he took a job just out of college that he thought could make life better for people like him: other farm boys who wanted more for their families than endless days in the fields and legendary stories about the storms that wiped out crops, the hot summers, and the myriad ways nature had taken it all. When he landed a director's role at an agricultural chemical company, he knew that his work mattered and that he had found a way to make a huge difference for families like his. He was happy for three decades—and then the company was purchased and resold three times in four years. Walter became disheartened as he was passed over for promotion after promotion. He had become a little like the farm, weathering one storm—one environmental change—after another.

Walter retired in place, doing just enough to get by and counting the days until his tenure was finally done. He thought no one noticed his level of disengagement—but everyone in the company knew he was unhappy and insecure. No one—not the human resources professionals, not the new senior leaders—wanted to call him out. He was a great guy and only a couple of years away from retirement, so they just left him alone. But it was a bad situation for both Walter and his coworkers.

The Heart: Walter happened to be on the team that went through a team coaching experience with one of our seasoned coaches. During the interview stage of the team work, the coach sensed he was holding back and asked him what it would take for him to show up and contribute his amazing ideas and strengths every day. Walter finally spoke up about what it was like to be passed over for promotions. In finding his voice, he experienced some deep-seated and long-forgotten emotions and rediscovered his passion for the work. He came to life for the first time in years. He remembered what had been missing not only in his work but in his life.

The No-Brainer: Identifying the things that had gone missing in his life, he reflected for a day on what he really wanted most, both in his job and his home. He wrote those things in a journal and began taking small actions to change his habits each day.

Have the Guts: Walter started working out each morning. He found new energy for his work. His wife noticed. His kids noticed. Those who stopped by his office on their way to lunch noticed. They were intrigued. Walter made a conscious decision to treat this work as he would the family farm. There was always a new season of planting on the horizon on the farm. It was time to (figuratively) plant again at work. He'd remembered the wisdom and zeal that had always been within him.

Walter sat with his human resources partner one day and explained an idea for how to transfer the company's legacy science to newer researchers. He helped frame needed leadership competencies for younger generations to cultivate adept and experienced managers. Instead of retiring within two years, Walter was promoted to a senior-level role and attended board meetings on occasion to share some of his insights about what products needed innovating.

The Path Back to Zealing Out: If you find you have been passed over for that key role or have retired mentally, look up and out. Find a way to contribute to those who come behind you. What would it take for you to be satisfied for another five or even ten years? Then engage the people around you who you think can help you create that type of environment.

6. Runners

The Bones: I put in the work to graduate at the top of my class for this? There is no such thing as a sure thing, a soul mate, or a perfect job. Disappointment is the norm. Didn't expect to become a wage slave working for "the man." I'm job hopping like I'm speed dating, and lowering my expectations to find any job that will pay the bills. I'm invisible at the office: Why am I never chosen?

The Skinny: Pat was a star athlete in college until he was benched with an injury in his junior year. He redirected his energies to his studies and graduated at the top of his class, always feeling the need to achieve any goal he set for himself. He moved into the MBA program at a prestigious university nearby and graduated with some internships under his belt and a great resumé. He was hired by his favorite business, a heritage brand company with expanding global reach, which could mean growth in leadership roles and lots of opportunities. This company had a track record of hiring graduates from the top of their class and loved former athletes in particular because the leadership liked to create internal competition for high performance. In fact, many former athletes had made their way to the top of the company over the organization's fifty years in business.

Pat quickly became a top sales performer but kept getting passed over for management positions and senior rep promotions. His boss, also a former athlete, told him to overcome any disappointment and "suck it up." Pat was told there would be other chances, but his boss avoided looking Pat in the eyes.

The Heart: Pat has a male life partner. He had not been open about his personal life at work because the guys on his sales team were much like the guys in his dorm room and on the baseball field. In the past, he had been the punch line of too many bad jokes and even subjected to brutal hazing. His rationale for keeping his sexuality a secret in the workplace? "What they don't know they won't hold against me or tease me about."

Pat was sure that revealing this truth about himself would be a huge risk in his conservative and competitive working environment. Then his partner developed a chronic illness that needed a higher level of care. The added complications of his personal life sent Pat over the edge. He was exhausted and burned out. He had no energy left for his job—or anything else. He decided to hire a coach.

One of the most interesting dynamics I have seen in two decades of coaching is that people at every level think they can separate or hide their personal lives from their work lives. All I have to say about that is, yeah, right! People know when the boss is having an affair. People know when something in a coworker's life—an illness, a change in child care arrangements—is difficult to manage or bear. Rest assured, your colleagues and friends at work know you are gay, and, for the most part, they really don't care if you are gay, straight, bisexual, transgender, or purple.

What people do care about is that you are competent and that you care as much as they do about the work that needs to get done to sustain the organization and everyone's livelihood. Although your personal life sometimes plays into how you are considered for that next promotion at work, it's not nearly as much of a factor as it was in the past.

"Pat, they already know you're gay," his coach told him. "What are you going to do to honor your relationship? There may be a short list of things no one really talks about, but everyone either knows this truth about you or senses that you are hiding something."

The No-Brainer: Pat decided to get help from the company's human resource manager to find the right language to let his boss know about the challenges he faced. He requested a move out of the East Coast division and into a new branch in a smaller town out west, where the environment supported his partner's health. He honored his partner by introducing him at the company picnic the following week as he said his goodbyes to long-term teammates.

To his surprise, Pat felt a kindness from others that he had not previously experienced. His colleagues were entirely supportive of his move and his partner. He took three weeks off to make the move, creating a base-camp-type retreat with his new home. His newfound confidence in being his authentic self at work helped Pat take the lead on several projects in the new branch; he was promoted to a leadership position on a rock star team. Feeling more optimistic and energetic than he had in a long time, Pat started working out again and tried out for the over-thirty baseball league in his new town. He now plays shortstop again three nights a week and is leadoff batter for a team who wears rainbow colors. Pat has a smile on his face and a happy word of encouragement for so many other people that his partner says his energy is too big to fit in their new condo these days. Both are healing nicely in every way, and Pat is happy he risked living more fully!

Have the Guts: Much is said and written about authenticity, but it is still one of the most difficult challenges any of us face— to remember our truths and honor those we love. Telling the truth right where you are is a bold thing to do. It may make you uncomfortable at first, but ultimately it will set you free. Are you willing to risk having things fall apart so you can start fresh in an environment that supports who you really are? What's the truth you really need to tell to come alive now?

The Path Back to Zealing Out: Look at yourself in the mirror tonight or tomorrow morning. Tell yourself a simple truth you have been keeping from others. Practice telling it until it becomes the undeniable thing that you have to honor. In the following days, weeks, and months, observe how you attract the circumstances to reveal your truth to others, then move into and live more fully in the truth of your life. Love and be open to love. Ask yourself this question and spend some time answering it: How good am I willing to have my life be, right now, right where I am?

7. Burnt-Out Superhero (Sometimes Known as *Mombie*)

The Bones. I'm putting in the time: 80–90 hour weeks, with 4:30 a.m. wake-up calls, is my new norm. Working around the clock for that promotion. So tired I'm cranky with everyone from my kids to my team. Neglecting my spouse in an effort to excel at work. Work–life balance is a joke. Just not enough of me to go around. And definitely not enough time for me.

The Skinny: The first person in and the last to leave every day at her high-wealth financial planning office, chief operating officer Jill found herself in a commuter family. Her office was three hundred miles from her husband and children and a forty-minute train ride from her weekday apartment. She was a visible thought leader, hired after the 2008 Wall Street debacle to help reestablish credibility at her global financial and investment firm. In her apartment in northern New Jersey, she arose each morning at 5:45 a.m. and rode a stationary bike for thirty minutes while she caught the news. She showered and drove twenty minutes to catch the train into New York City, then stopped at Starbucks for a double shot of espresso and a PowerBar before she breezed by the building's security guards on the way to her office. As soon as she found her way to her corner office, she was on international Skype conferences discussing the opening stocks in Asian and European markets.

Because Jill was so visible, she had to always look her best, so she found couture designers and hairdressers who would meet her in the office at scheduled times each month. One of her assistants was also a stylist who met her early each day to make sure she was fit for the conferences and TV cameras. She was the only woman on the large and growing steering committee and answered to the board for the operations of the firm. Keeping up with her calendar took two executive assistants and a chief of staff. Her private plane was always ready to whisk her to any number of destinations.

Although she spoke slowly and deliberately to her chief operating council, confident in her understanding of market changes, it was clear to those who were close to her that she was spinning out beneath that demure demeanor. Jill was close to the breaking point.

The Heart: Jill's twelve-year-old daughter, Adrienne, the youngest of her three children, began having grand mal seizures for which doctors couldn't find a cause. Jill left three key meetings over the course of ten days. The private jet rushed her to hospital bedsides just long enough to make sure that everything was okay and that her husband could handle the pressure of tending to the three kids and their schedules while also managing the growing list of specialists that the family had on speed dial. Jill's husband was growing more and more distant and blamed her for Adrienne's health challenges. "If you'd just spend more time at home, the seizures will stop," he told her. Family tension was building, and Jill's sixteen-year-old son stopped talking to her.

Jill faced a life-altering choice: stay the course for a globe-trotting superwoman career that supported her political aspirations and that could enable her to influence major policy changes, or reconnect with her family and find ways to reduce her travel and the demands of her work. Family had always come first but, until now, work and home had always seemed easy to balance.

The No-Brainer: Jill walked through her home in Virginia and looked into the faces of people who appeared to be strangers. Pictures of family events she'd missed covered the fridge. She walked into Adrienne's room, sat on the edge of the bed, and started to cry. Jill called a family conference, and as the family grumbled their way into the living room, she sat for a long time without saying anything. She was having a hard time finding the words to communicate her truest feelings. Finally, her eldest son asked, "Mom, do you have something to say, or should we go back to what we were doing?"

"I have something to say." Taking a deep breath, she said simply, "I love you all so, so much. You are the most important people in my life. I cannot apologize enough or tell you again how much you mean to me, but I can show you. I am willing to completely give up my career now if that is what we all think is important. Before I do, I want to outline some options. Let's figure out together what decision I need to make about my career." Jill outlined everything she had considered and described what she really liked about her job: the people she served, her political ambitions, the magazine articles she'd authored. She explained that although what she did was important, it wasn't nearly as meaningful to her as being there for her kids as they navigated their teenage years.

Jill's family helped her come up with a career compromise, something Jill hadn't thought of before. It was time for Mom to move her second home from New Jersey into NYC to shorten her daily commute and for the kids and Dad to move within a short train ride of the city so Jill and her family could see each other more often. Jill's kids were willing to change schools and have a family adventure if it meant they could all be together more. The boys could excel at sports in their new school and Adrienne would be near better health care specialists. They were proud of their mother and wanted her to be successful. "Mom, I want to have a career like you some day," Adrienne said. "You have to show me the way. If you leave now, we will never know what you might become."

Have the Guts: Be willing to choose according to your biggest, most important personal values. Doing so is akin to a reckoning. You have to sort through the conundrums and tribal conversations about what's "right" and start aligning your choices with your values, moment to moment during your day. You can torment yourself with either/or decisions or shift the conversation to both/and conversations. What compromises can you make that don't involve sacrificing your career or your family? What is the best way for you to honor your goals while valuing the people you love?

The Path Back to Zealing Out: Start your mornings with breathing exercises instead of breathless activities. If you need to meditate or make your way to a yoga class to begin to find the space and time to just breathe, then do so. Slow your mind speed down so that your choices are clear. Make a set of at least five rituals every morning. These can be as simple as stretching when getting out of bed, breathing deeply for ten minutes, mentally acknowledging the one thing you are most grateful for when your eyes open, eating breakfast, singing a song in the shower, kissing your family good morning, breathing deeply on your commute to the office, turning off the radio for ten minutes of your commute, drinking hot herbal or cold teas instead of espresso, and greeting your colleagues meaningfully at the beginning of the day. Shifting from breathless to breathing opens up your capacity and energizes you. You are building the ability to love and care for others and to see a greater good in all that you do. Every day is a beginning.

Inhale. Exhale. Repeat *as often as needed*.

You Are Getting the Picture Now: What's Next?

Can you relate to any of the individuals in the previous stories? Have you ever found yourself on a zombie team and working for a zombie boss? Do you long for the good old days? Or perhaps you simply run from one job to the next, no workplace or job ever satisfying you. Do you feel disembodied and disenfranchised? Most of us can relate to one of these scenarios at some time or other in our work lives. I have personally played the role of the Superhero given that I have a great capacity for work and creativity. Many enthusiastic leaders who are not listed specifically here have their own inner journeys that differ from those listed here but contain similar challenges of head and heart. The journey to self-awareness and dancing back into the light is a path we all may take at some point in our careers.

Breaking free from feeling anything but amazing is a daily endeavor. Finding yourself in the wrong cultural environment, taking the wrong job, comparing yourself to the person who got the job you wanted, or losing your temper or your patience can all lead to your clawing your way out of the darkness. Yet, when you stop to take account of what is really going on in your world, you may be closer to becoming a joy-filled zealot than you might have previously imagined. Wherever you are in your journey from zombie to zealot, from surviving to thriving, you have the power to climb out of any hole in your career, and come back to life. With motivation and hard work, you can free yourself from the zombie virus, and call your spirit back into its fullest expression.

Remember Who You Are: You and Your Purpose

If you can relate to any of the previous stories and feel you're not on the right track, you have, I hope, gained some insights about ways to correct your course. Tired of pursuing other people's goals rather than your own, you can get clear about what you don't want anymore and begin to reinvent yourself and pursue your dreams. You may feel a sense of urgency to dig deep: to remember who you are and what you want to do. It's now time to find your way onto a playing field that is big enough for your soul—back to the bigger game you are here on Earth to play.

Moving Through the Stages of Remembering

Dr. Carolyn Myss has described three types of consciousness in her book *Sacred Contracts*: tribal consciousness, individual consciousness, and divine consciousness.[6] Based on Myss's work and my own understanding of these concepts which has deepened over the years, I would describe each level of consciousness as follows:

1. Tribal consciousness – viewing the world through the lens of your family of origin, your culture, and society, often unconsciously seeing things from the perspective of these groups and their needs and desires. Simply stated: "What others want and need from you."
2. Individual consciousness – viewing the world through your own unique lens as an individual; realizing you

are separate from your family, culture, and society, you choose your own path and see the world through a unique lens, recognizing your own values, needs and desires. Simply stated: "What you want."

3. Divine consciousness – viewing the world through the lens of a larger and more awakened state of consciousness, you witness life through a more open lens, including the universe in a state of expansion; seeing things from the perspective of your Spirit, higher self, God, whatever you consider the ultimate source of your power. The simple question you heed, with heightened awareness is: "What wants me?"

When I work with leaders, we typically move through these three stages of consciousness as part of the process of remembering their true purpose and aligning that with how they team with others. However, I rarely call out each stage they are in as it occurs. We just explore where these leaders are focused and what they are challenged by, and I point out their patterns or archetypes until they become clear about who they really are and where they play in those three levels of conscious development. My goal is to always leave them playing in the light, integrating each stage of consciousness so that they can live authentically, work wholeheartedly, ignite their teams, and stay aligned as they partner with others.

It isn't easy to be completely authentic or to work from a state in which we are most connected with the divine without having others—our tribe or company or society or egos—want to limit us, save us, or control us. Most of our experiences have indicated that it is much easier to hide out, fit in, and be nice, and we do so at all costs—literally. Running and hiding costs us everything—our self-worth, our happiness, our loves, our lives. We sell out, we settle, we dumb down, and we stay in our fear zone because shining authentically has caused us pain in the past. Yet, for those who know this is their work—to be light, live in grace, and illuminate the brilliance of others right where they are—part of the deal is risking the loss of something you may be attached to like a love interest, a position or role, or even a wardrobe or car. Every challenge you face right now is preparing you to come into your power more fully.

Our task and the big question remains: How do you remember? That is, how do you embody your true self and purpose by learning to identify where you are in the spaces or gaps between each of these levels of understanding and awareness?

First, take a few minutes to think through three reflective questions:

1) What do others need and want from me?
2) What do I really want now?
3) What wants me? What calls to me? What voice can I no longer ignore?

Journal them in the following space provided below each question or in a notebook, or just think about them. Notice the level of consciousness you play out in your career. Are you giving others what they want but sacrificing yourself, or are you clear about what you want and asking yourself the bigger question about what you might do that would give you complete joy?

1. *What do others need from me now? Who am I for others?* (tribal consciousness)

First, answer this question: *What do others want or need from you?* Do you prioritize the needs of others over your true values, or do you allow yourself to get sucked into groups focused on negativity and apathy? Birds of a feather flock together, and zombies beget zombies. Look to the demands others make of you and how you deal with them. Surrounded by zombies? Find or organize a tribe of zealots to energize and inspire you instead.

Next, determine who you are for others. What are you known for in your group of friends? Are you the host, the entertainer, the comedian, the sage, the lover, the mom, the royal, the instigator, the peacemaker, or something else? Whoever you are for others is a big clue into the way you play this game of being fully human. And although you are more than one dimension, there is a way you show up in the world that is most natural and gives you the most joy or sense of satisfaction.

What do others want and need from you? Jot your answer here.

2. *What do you want most now?* (individual consciousness: what I want!)

When we embrace our individual consciousness, we move away from our tribe of origin or that tribe that keeps us playing smaller so that we fit in and address their needs with our work. We grow and evolve as we seek what is personally, soulfully important and meaningful—what we really want to manifest to be successful in our own measures. Want to be a chef instead of a finance director? Want to be a coach instead of a burnt out manager? When we tune into our individual consciousness, we are able to recognize the power of changing our mind-set, our thinking. We feel in control. And we are able to create a new way forward, one small step or giant leap at a time.

What do you want most now? Jot your answer here.

3. *Who are you really? (What voice is calling me? Where is the reckoning for that voice and how do I pay attention?)* (divine consciousness: what wants me!)

Life often asks us to surrender to our highest and best contribution by giving us something that we don't want: a job loss, a disconnection such as divorce from a toxic relationship or a broken spiritual connection, or an illness that demands new awareness so we find our way back to the right work. If you accept that you are divine and more than flesh and bones, it is easier to see that you came from and return to divinity. (If you find yourself in a tough spot, you might request of the universe to "please let the lessons be easy ones.") That you are in part divine is also a great perspective to hold when you seek to answer these questions: What is really calling me? What wants me now that I cannot ignore any longer? What is that work?

From a place of divine consciousness, our work and play become the same to us. We lose track of time. We have revelations, learn, and assimilate quickly. We feel connected. We witness the light in others because we experience light and love ourselves. We witness miracles and pay attention to subtle whispers of wisdom from a greater source that we might otherwise miss. We are masters of abundance and generous with all of our natural gifts and physical resources. This level of paying attention, of becoming authentic, gives us power.

Who are you really? Jot your answer here.

After you have answered these questions, I have two more coaching questions for you to consider in order to deepen the understanding you are gaining as you remember who you really are:

4. Where do you want to play most fully now that you are remembering?

5. What are you waiting for?

You can't expect to arrive at your destination if you don't know where you want to go. GPS doesn't have directions for "someplace better than this one!" You know you don't want to be a zombie, so take some time to think about what you really, really, really want to be and what ignites you. Remember what first inspired you to step out or take a risk once upon a time. Then, consider this formula:

Who I Am for Others + What I Really Want + Heeding My Calling + Remembering Who I Am = the Bigger Game

Now write your own version of this formula here, drawing on what you captured earlier in this chapter.

When you put these pieces together, what do you discover? Talk to a coach. Journal your thoughts and questions. Get moving! Remember who you are and you will be ready to find ways to reconnect.

ReConnect

Connection is humanity's way
Of energetically evolving and growing
Together
Witnessing the light in others allows them
To see themselves as we do, a most powerful reflection in our eyes
It is time, beyond time, to embody
The force and power that is ours to see the best in others as we
Reawaken, Remember, Reconnect.

DJ's Journal, November 2015

The Third Path Back to the Light

ReConnect

Are you ready to fully *reconnect*: integrating conscious awareness, intuitive knowing, and courageous action? Reconnecting is the part of the journey back into the light where your spirit's wisdom and your physical senses blend together. You have awakened to the truth within and now you will learn to transcend or shift old ways of working. You recognize your divine nature in everyday challenges and understand that you are enough and that your work matters, so you now choose where you will apply your energy and you can more consistently play and stay in the "zealot zone."

Reconnecting occurs as you integrate your inner and outer worlds, plugging the real you into the real world, and discovering the ignition of spirit and experience of zeal that accompanies that. On this path, you know yourself, you believe in yourself, and you can translate that self-understanding and confidence into day-to-day activity, experimenting with new ways of doing things and opening your heart and mind to others as you contribute your best to your team and the larger missions you serve.

Consider the act of *reconnection* as a way of assimilating and aligning your primary energy centers:

- your heart center – (your feelings and ability to connect or relate)
- your mind – (your ability to think and create)
- your will or instinctive center – (your ability to speak your truth and to call forth courage when it is most needed).

When you are reconnected, these three centers are fully aligned; it becomes easy to pay attention to your inner wisdom, with the voice of your spirit as a trusted guide. Gaining that level of integration is the key to understanding that your outer world is a reflection of your inner world, meaning that what you believe and hold true, you will tend to manifest in many ways.

When you are aligned and have this sense of wellbeing, you are connected with who you really are. You also connect differently with those around you—another biggie on the path back to the light. You see your connection with the environment as a responsibility. You are at one with all that is important in your world. You come back to your centers again and again as you navigate all of life's challenges.

You **Re**Connect and come back to life more fully. You come back to work full of life. You consciously choose your path, and stay more at ease in the "zealot zone."

I once coached a business leader who was a retired professional basketball player. He recounted an experience of ignition—complete zeal—when he was in the zone that brings this concept to life:

> I had this game where I felt like I was one with everything around me—aware of what was outside of me, as if I had

fully embodied it—there was no separation between me and the basketball, me and the goal, me and other players, me and the fans. We were all a part of one energetic body. My performance felt like it was suspended in space and time. I was superhuman in that moment in time—aware that this game and this life were much bigger than me alone. I drew my source of energy from this hyper connection. I made almost all of my shots and was the MVP in that game.

My client went on to explain that having this experience happens in sports to almost every professional athlete at some point in their careers and that it is rare air: "Yet it is such a euphoric high that athletes rigorously seek the experience." Getting back to that experience is aspirational, but a handful of players learned to connect and be so fully present that this feeling, this high, became their driver for success. In fact, "the feeling is so compelling that we practice like crazy to feel that way again—to feel that this is my night, my time to be the star, another chance to embody the experience of the zone—and to zeal out!"

Workplace zealots breathe the same rare air of the star athlete who plays in the zone. They experience that level of connection, and they will practice and rigorously (even religiously) work to find new ways to connect to that feeling as often as possible. Are you curious about what it takes to reconnect and find zeal in your own work?

Working zealots—those who have *reconnected*—thrive on the energy of being in their own zone. When you find the zone, you feel not only like you are one with everything around you but, in a way, as if you have been liberated to be yourself, wholeheartedly. You start living vibrantly each day of the week instead of waiting for the weekend so that you can breathe again. This sense of well-being is translated to the brain as a message from a happy spirit:

This is why I am alive—what I was put here for.

I BELONG HERE, now.

This is my right work. I am of service and fulfilled.

Your Career Path Is Synonymous with Your Spiritual Path

When you are in the zone, you see every obstacle as a challenge that makes you spiritually stronger, galvanizes your will, and requires you to innovate and create new solutions in your life. You realize that every day is a gift and that learning and living through your lessons is how you keep score of the vital aspects of your game.

Look back at some of your toughest career challenges and you might find your most noble challengers were actually your soul mates: people who drove you crazy enough so that you set a boundary or grew in some new and unexpected way. One of the purest distinctions between zealots and zombies is that zombies don't get that the lessons in life are spiritual. And remember, zealots don't struggle; they play. Have you ever watched the Dalai Lama laugh as he talks about his exile from Tibet? He smiles and speaks simply about everything, including the toughest, most heartbreaking events of his life outside of his country of origin. He doesn't dismiss rational thinking. Rather, he can analyze, observe, and learn just like everyone else, understanding more than most that gaining perspective and creatively coping with the obstacles he encounters in life carve new paths for joy.

I would categorize Steve Jobs as a zealot: He so embodied Apple that we cannot think of the company, the Mac, the iPod, the iPad, and the iPhone without picturing him in our minds. It wasn't that he was consumed with the notion of excellence; rather, he embodied it. Consumed, in this case, meaning to be eaten up with a notion, focused in way that doesn't allow for innovation. Embodied, meaning that the idea is integrated and expanded, residing in your being as an expression of you and yet it is connected to something beyond you—bigger than you alone.

Jobs was criticized for the way he managed people from time to time, but no one doubted his ability to produce magical experiences with the products he brought into the world. It was as if he asked the universe, "What's next?" and then caught the answer right before anyone else realized we needed Apple's help to advance how we communicate. He created a field of play because he could enthusiastically convey to his team the potential impact of Apple's innovation on the world. People like him (remember the law of attraction: "that which is like itself is drawn" or "birds of a feather flock together") surrounded Jobs, wanting to tap into his zeal and to help him achieve his ambitious aspiration for art and excellence. People longed for ways to reconnect after the birth of the Internet, and Jobs gave us the needed innovation.

The Neural Path to Happiness!

The word *reconnecting* in the context of neuroscience means that you are consciously connecting new ideas as you come online again, building happiness one strand of reprogramming at a time for yourself. Much is written these days about neuroplasticity and neuroscience, including biofeedback, which in its simplest form is the study of how we learn, program our brains, and build on recognition and memory. By experiencing new places, new languages, or new moves in a dance, among other things, we fire synapses in our brains that tack those new experiences onto the older ones. Our brilliant internal computer connects the dots between the old things we know—dancing, hiking, language, eating—and the new skills we learn—"this new dance is Zumba," "I am taking a new path on this hike," "*lune* is the French word for the moon, which reminds me of the English word *lunar*," "hey, this Cuban sandwich is like a supercharged grilled cheese."

Building onto something we already know creates a new mental map of possibilities. Embodying these new concepts comes from taking the dance class, listening to the language or immersing ourselves in it, or singing that new song until it rolls around in our brain as our new favorite until we consciously choose this new thing—a novel language, movement, or song—as the path we intentionally select. The more we use that portion of our brain in a focused and selective way, the more the neural pathways will develop in the direction of the experience we consistently seek. Happiness becomes a choice.

So if you have been spiraling down at work because of the chaos caused by recent changes on the job and you have focused (as humans do) on protective, negative internal dialogue and consequences, it might take some rethinking to spiral back up. It might take a little bit of practice and some time to choose happiness as your state of being each day.

Know this: Gratitude for what you have now and what is working will help you accelerate your journey back into your happy zone, to live a more "zoetic" (peaceful and fulfilling) life. If you begin there, you will start from a firmer foundation than your negative bias or self-talk.

There is a video circulating on the web and in social media of a man dancing on the lawn at a concert by himself. A few minutes into his dance, a few others bravely move their feet. It likely wasn't his intention to transform a solo dance into a full-on rave. Yet his passion and power were so compelling that his moves invited followers and influenced others to stand up and sway, surrounding this man on the lawn. The small group became an expanding circle until it consumed the entire lawn. The same thing is true for people who love their work. They explore, they risk, they move, and others take a stand and join in: The circle expands. Their engagement becomes contagious—happily contagious—until the whole place is filled with people who are intentionally and often intensely engaged, swaying together to a new beat.

Zealots are courageous scouts in ways that some consider silly. They can lead a movement with no concern for how big it becomes or whether they get full credit. They do what they do because they cannot imagine not doing it, whatever that "it" may be. Their feet move to the rhythm in their lives.

Zombies don't hear the music and can't dance.

They trudge.

They go to their graves with their real gifts and their music still in them.

Dare You to Become Maddeningly Happy: Double Dog Dare You

The universe seems to respond faster to those whose frequencies are cranked up. Has anyone ever asked you to "cheer down"? Have you ever been told that your enthusiasm is contagious or that you are maddeningly happy?

If not, why not?

For most people, what's holding them back is simply fear. Maybe you're worried about debt or feel like you have to postpone joy until you get better organized, better prepared, or more in control of your life. Maybe your spiritual longings keep getting pushed to the back room in your inner sanctuary. Maybe you think extreme joy is only for other people—people who have it all together.

When coaching a female executive who was happy most of the time but stressed to the max, I asked her, "Just how good are you willing to have your life be?" She stewed in silence for a long time before she said, "I do feel I'm happy. I just keep waiting for the other shoe to drop. I am afraid I will fall into that same pattern from my past where I screw things up or sabotage my happiness." Here's the thing: That type of fear is merely an internal dialogue you are having with yourself. It is a mind-set, not a reality. Let's explore a few examples from the archetypes we created as illustration of internal dialogues that keep people disconnected from their zeal.

Sold Out:

Inner Dialogue of Fear: "I have to stay in this job at all costs. I am miserable here but I just have to suck it up or else my family and I won't be able to keep living the good life. Or we might not even be able to survive."

Reality: "If I choose to, I can make changes that will allow me to enjoy this job or a new job altogether. I can and will make a living to support myself and my family."

If you are among those who sold out, you are likely staying in the wrong job at all costs because you believe that you *have* to. The reality is that you have choices, alternatives, and the power to make changes.

Runners:

Inner Dialogue of Fear: "I can't be happy at this job so I have to leave it, and the sooner the better. Surely, something out there is better than this."

Reality: "I have the power to make changes within myself that will allow me to be happier at my current job or the next job that I pursue."

If you are regularly running to the next position, next job, or next industry over, always thinking that the problem is "them" not "you," you've given away your power to external sources rather than understanding that you have the power to change you and that can make all the difference.

Zombie Boss:

Inner Dialogue of Fear: "My boss is going to fire me or ruin my reputation so I can never get another job in this town again."

Reality: "My boss is operating in ways that aren't constructive. I have the choice to communicate with him to improve the situation and/or seek job opportunities elsewhere. I have so much to offer my employer and trust that I will be able to make that known, either here or at my next opportunity."

It's easy to feel angry, resentful or afraid when you have a zombie boss; it's even natural. Shifting those negative emotions to ones of empowerment and self-belief will give you the confidence to remedy the situation.

It's easy for these mental myths to seem like reality—because you're protecting yourself or you're not risking greatness for whatever excuse you give. It is easier to hang on to the protective thoughts rolling around, taking up head space so you feel protected, and, before long you come to believe that these thoughts are true. They aren't. They are simply musings on former experiences or fear—why else would you need to be protected? Many of us choose to hang on to these old ways of thinking, these mind-sets, as a means of protecting ourselves, yet what's really happening is that we are paralyzing ourselves. Stop thinking like that. Your thoughts become a part of your reality. You can choose better thoughts and manifest better experiences. You can adopt a mind-set of possibility and start from a position of happiness. A few simple rituals can help reprogram your brain from zombie to zealot.

Dr. Cindi Ackrill is a stress management expert and a member of our coaching team. Cindi is also part of the faculty for Pyramid's Healthcare Coaching Institute program and has studied neurobiofeedback and the impact of stress in our bodies. Her focus in our classes is to teach people to adopt simple rituals of self-talk to reprogram their brains. When you brush your teeth each morning, for example, claim that you are going to have a great day. Try it. It always brings me a big foamy smile, so trust me when I say that it is worth risking. Can you imagine 70 million workers getting their day started with this same ritual every morning? We can start a movement!

The first step to change begins with identifying and proclaiming what you want to experience. There are other simple techniques to get started too:

- *Stay, computer, stay!* Tell your computer to stay as if it were your dog. See the work patiently waiting to become a priority tomorrow. Let go of your guilt (that's a self-imposed injury) about having dinner with your family and making that Little League game. Go play!
- *Recharge your phone so you can recharge your life.* Put your phone in its cradle or in charge mode when you arrive home and step away from it. Remember what it was like to actually have a life untethered? Then let the messages and the e-mails be sweet little surprises when you have taken time for yourself and people you care about after work. When it's time to pick that phone back up, use it

to call others once in a while rather than to simply send a text. That's the power of real connection. Recharge your phone and recharge your life!

- *Go barefoot!* Touch the earth with your bare feet each day, even if you have to move some snow. You are electromagnetic, and grounding yourself is important for your health and well-being, which are critical for energy to perform your work.

- *Breathe, inhale, and exhale.* Repeat as often as needed. Every time I write this, I laugh out loud. When I wrote my autobiography titled *Mystic Grits: A Southern Girl's Journey to Wisdom*, a young female friend queried, "*Mystic Grits?* Are you one of those mystics, shaman, yogis or something? Do you teach people to breathe in Jesus and blow out Satan?" After I picked myself up from the deck of the boat where I'd collapsed in laughter, I replied, "Something like that." We are a breathless society. Breathing is essential for reconnecting to our health, our heart, and our best thinking: our mindfulness. So you can breathe in any peaceful, positive, affirming thought or belief that resonates for you and blow out any thought, feeling, pattern of behavior, or personal drama that doesn't serve you.

- *Take 3!* Look for three things that make you happy on the current job, in your home, or with your family and focus on only those things for one week. Notice what changes!

These rituals are easy enough to do, right? Remember the importance of neural pathways in your practice and get moving! Choose and practice happiness!

Truth and Dare

If you simply aspire to park your cynicism somewhere before entering the pearly gates of the home office and can't imagine living and working as an enthusiastic zealot, you are not alone. Yet, this call to at least play with the notion of being exuberant as a way of life is worth exploration, as it just may enable you to successfully calibrate where you are on your path and lead you to where you really want to go.

We humans are conditioned to experience a negative bias. We have lived in fear of many things—some of them myths—and we love our life so much that we are apt to want to protect it at all costs—to survive—even if we are miserable and have lost faith in our current situations. We hang on to the hope that things will look up, will get better, if only this or that will fall into place, rather than through our own taking of action.

As you cultivate and clarify your purpose, discovering who you are and how you want to work and contribute (as we explored together in the ReMember section of the book), you may find that the path back to your center, your spirit, surprisingly conveys you back to life, and you are liberated, seeing joy and possibilities rather than only limitations. You begin the day happier and end that same way: with a smile on your face. That is the first step up and out on your path to reconnect with your inner zeal.

Most of us experience a dance between exuberance and the zed-head state of the zombie as we move in and out of our different roles at work, at home, and in life. We stay closer to a satisfied state when we are in the right career or the right role and everything else is in place; otherwise, we spend time chasing satisfaction, wanting more, and never feeling we are or have enough. Even this notion of job satisfaction can feel like a stretch for most employees these days, but you may be closer than you think to zealing out! Here are some clues that you might be well on your way. Check out this list of characteristics to see if you are on the path to zealing out. Do any of these apply to you? If so, exciting! If not, do not judge yourself…today is a new day and you are ready to begin. This list can be something to aspire to and to operationalize.

Do you . . .

- wake up without an alarm clock and begin the day with exercise, meditative breathing, or quiet reflection to mentally, spiritually, and physically prepare for the work you will do?
- give gratitude for both the day and the people you serve with your efforts?
- feel present to the needs of your family and affirm your partner, expressing love and positivity before going off to experience your workday?
- commute to work with the sound that keeps you present, whether that's music, your child's laughter, the wind, the playful banter of friends in the carpool, or silence?
- enjoy the people you work with and exchange energy and inspiration by sharing challenges and insights?

- have a leader or mentor from whom you can regularly seek guidance, support, and wisdom?
- communicate fully and take ownership of miscommunications and mistakes?
- love the people around you?
- make the lives of the people around you easier through your words, actions, and demonstrations of your commitment?
- care deeply and sincerely about the small things that make a big difference?
- live beautifully in the right environment with the right people?
- believe in and demonstrate the law of attraction: Like attracts like?

If you answered yes to even some of these indicators, you are on the path. You're already more zealot than zombie. You are closer to unleashing new possibilities and reconnecting with your zeal than you might have realized, without even taking early retirement. If you answered no, don't worry. Pick any three of the items on this list and start engaging in them. Watch as the zeal begins to flow for you.

Zealots Are Contagious Too!

Being or experiencing the feeling of being a victim to circumstance is no fun for anyone. Staying in that place endangers our souls because there we give others the power in our lives. Stagnating in zombiehood costs people their health, their lives, and their experience of being fully alive and present in the earth game. Not that you will care too much, but it also costs your company millions of actual dollars in health care and lost business opportunities that might have given you more resources to do great work. Lucky for all of us, just as becoming a zombie is a viral threat, becoming a zealot is a happy contagion.

We have seen the impact of happy people on each other in many companies. There are some great places to work in the world, and more companies are adopting strategies to help people fully engage and become more satisfied while in the office. In one of Pyramid Resource's client companies, our team-coaching process changed the culture in just such a direction: Within six months, absenteeism was reduced by 60 percent because people tuned in and cared about how they were contributing to the bottom line. How? We changed the work game by guiding a team through the Team Advantage™ process I created as a foundation for team coaching.

Initially, this team was very skeptical about Team Advantage™ and looked at it as just another attempt to initiate change, one more "flavor of the month." The first day of the kickoff workshop was challenging, and the team struggled to come up with a goal for their game. Day 2 of the kickoff workshop provided a breakthrough for the team. They decided on an extraordinary goal that would focus on team empowerment and engagement and created strategic drivers around staff development, staff behavior, attendance, and alignment of policy and procedures. Their skepticism about time commitment was allayed by an exercise known as the "fast forward focus," which identified all of the barriers to their success in implementing their plan. They realized that there were no obstacles that they could not overcome.

The ongoing coaching sessions became the most valuable aspect of Team Advantage™. There was nearly 100 percent participation in every session and a renewed sense of commitment from the team. Their separate operating silos started to break down, and communication among the management team reached a new level of efficiency. Probably the most significant shift was the transformation in the primary focus of the team from managing day-to-day work to leading their direct reports and encouraging their teams to explore process improvements. By making leadership the focus of their work, they empowered their teams and each other.

This was a huge return on investment and productivity, but, more important, the group found enjoyment in working with each other. Those friendships didn't just bring more energy to the company: They created a web of relationships based on trust. There's a lot more at stake when the person you might be letting down is a treasured colleague instead of a zoned-out zombie. The company culture shifted from fear based and stuck in nostalgia to a passionate team whose members valued one another and incorporated a spirit of play into their daily work. On this team, people wanted to come to work to be a part of what was going on. The virus of unhappiness was eradicated, and a mind-set of healthy change was sustainable. The contrast was dramatic enough that the CEO quipped, "Why aren't we doing this for all of our teams?"

The company won an award for best practice at a national convention. We trained internal culture champions to drive the Team Advantage™ process, and more of the teams in this organization are now being coached to play a bigger game and measure the impact on employees and customers.

For some of you, reframing negative situations on your path to embodied zeal can help you keep sight of the big picture. "I may dislike the work I have and the extra hours I'm putting in, but I know that the bonus I will receive will pay a year of college tuition, and I don't need to do this forever." This technique may help get you through rough spots, but don't let a lifetime go by living a story that you settled for instead of selecting. You deserve a zoetic life, and you are always the author of your own story. A situation can't undo you, but your reactions to a situation can.

Each of Us Has a Journey

It would be so much easier if someone could just hand us a roadmap and tell us where to put our energies to discover our life's calling and vocation. But don't mistake a lack of written directions for a lack of guidance or inspiration. It's all there waiting to be tapped into: It's a matter of asking and listening. Throw in measures of patience, faith, trust, and enthusiasm and you are on your way. Your spirit and the universe want you to succeed; set an intention to find your path and you will be given the answers, sometimes as a soulful whisper, and sometimes as a loud clang and disruption.

If there is one characteristic that I see in all of those who are most successful, it is *enthusiasm* for what they do. Once asked by an employer what one quality contributed to my success as a broadcast manager, I responded, "everyday enthusiasm." Work and play for me are same, same, same! I love what I do. That continues to be the case. Belief and trust have been part of the equation, too. Learning to believe in myself and the unfolding of things around me has worked for me and my team, and I have seen it work for my clients who trust that even if they didn't get that position they longed for, there was something better around the corner, something that fit and lifted them to a bigger game. We are not superheroes for finding our path when we do; we are actually just ordinary people who are consciously following a particular way of living, trusting that conscious choice in our work and lives transcends the daily challenges.

> Every step you have ever taken has brought you to this place.
>
> —Seen on a t-shirt in Stowe, Vermont

I love that t-shirt quote!

Every step you take is foundational for where you can go next. Your path is always a choice: day-to-day and moment-to-moment. Each step is your choice, even if and when you trudge unconsciously. Maybe you're not proud of some of the steps you've taken on your path. Welcome to humanity. We all have stumbled. It's time to stop judging and comparing. Wounds are your story until they become your resources. Forgive yourself for the past and start transforming your future by noticing the steps you take and the choices you make today. If you are to become fully present, you will want to claim each choice you make and each step you take as if it is "just for today." Your future is created that way... one step at a time. By reconnecting with your best self and your zeal, you can drop the zombie routine and focus on what gets you moving forward with consciousness, a compelling vision for how much fun you could have, and a joyful spirit.

Everyday enthusiasm. I have started most of my days for as long as I have been alive in a happy state. It's a blessing to feel that way and I want to share it with others. When I bounced out of bed and to the breakfast table as a child, my dad used to say, "Here comes happy!" I've also had enough experiences to learn to trust that when I was unhappy, happy would roll around again.

You can practice this trust, too. Find an ounce of happiness each morning, even if you have to fake it at first. Make a contribution, no matter how small, by being of service to others. If your barista seems grumpy, give 'em a smile as you order. If you're running through the drive-through, call the attendants serving you by their name and thank them when they throw your bag of food at you. Look into the eyes of others on your train and silently bless them—or just simply see them. After the events of September 11, 2001, when the world came to a complete halt for a minute and we were all paying attention to each other, it was common to see people gratefully look into each other's eyes as if to say, "I am here. We are here."

Honoring each other is so important.

It's time to reconnect. It's time to get out of our heads and be aware of the blessings and humanity around us. Notice when you're wallowing in what isn't working and shift your focus to the things that are. Do you have food for breakfast? Yahoo! Have a family that loves you? Yippee! Have friends at work? Care for them, tell them what you most appreciate! You get the picture. A zealot finds joy and beauty in the day-to-day journey.

If you are in a job too wrong for you to even fake satisfaction, then find something you can tolerate as a way of serving others until you make your way to the thing that calls to you. Get involved in changing a social problem through community service programs. When you focus on serving others, your attention moves from your problems to the realization that you have the power to manifest or attract more good. My mantra during the most challenging times of my life was simply this: "The good that comes to me creates good for others." I still practice this silently whenever I am scared about the monthly revenue projections or the stock market. In my practice, opportunities come knocking every day, if I am paying enough attention to see and catch them.

Mantra, Oh, Mantra

Your mantra is a daily practice of mindfulness or a silent prayer meant only for you—a reminder of your power and potential and a way for you to reconnect with your zeal at any time of day or night. It can be a single world or an entire phrase. Often this can be just a word you choose to guide you through the year. Sometimes it is a phrase or your grandmother's kitchen table wisdom, "if you aren't having fun, you aren't doing it right."

Find a word, phrase or idea that can be a reminder that you can find your joy in your daily journey and path. This is your personal rallying cry and will help reprogram those neural pathways. Repeat it to yourself every day: in the morning, before you go to bed, and whenever you find yourself falling into the zombie trap of self-pity and negative thinking. Your mantra is a wake-up call to joy. Take some time to contemplate and write it down below. Feel free to write a few versions until you feel you have found the right one for you for now—and change it when you desire.

Contagions on the Path: Impression Management is a Surefire Spiral to Zombification!

If you're stuck in zombie mode, it's likely you put on a mask every day when you step out the door on your way to work. That role you step into limits you. Reconnecting with the divine mystery demands you throw aside those limits and embrace all the parts of yourself—at home, at work, and everywhere you move through the world.

When we pour our energy into maintaining an external image of perfection, we are operating out of fear. If you look behind any type of fear, it typically can be traced back to one of three things: death of our ego, identity, or physical death. Those are the things that stop us. Fortunately, there is an alternative to living in the domain of fear: living in the domain of love. The ego's job is to keep us safe from harm. It is constantly going off in our heads about what we had better do or not do, and it is that little voice of judgment that keeps us from dancing even when we feel the music and want to move. It can keep us from taking bold leaps of faith to do what is most right for our soul. Giving way to ego demands we kill off some part of ourselves and sacrifice living authentically. I'm asking you to push past that, and I am living proof that you can. Connect with your passion and, if you must, thank your ego for sharing its concerns and then politely say, "shut up/be quiet—this voice, this fear, is not serving me right now." Then, get moving. Tap into the thing you were put on this earth to do.

To cope in a crazy world, we must come to terms with the notion that we are connected to, well, everything. Many of my clients come to me to grow to a new level or to become great with people. Some seek coaching because they're having difficulty with careers that feel dead-end or stifling; some have bosses that are breaking their spirit, and regret having taken the career path they now follow. One critical question that I ask those clients who feel disheartened is this, "When are you going to work in a way that is big enough for your spirit?"

I pose this question to those who are happy but need to stretch, just as I pose it to those who seem most unhappy. What's so important about this question? I'm not asking when you'll find the right job, or the perfect boss, or the exact fit for your skills and needs. I'm asking when *you* are going to work in a way that is big enough for your spirit. *You* are the person who can break free from the zombie mold. *You* are the person who has to reconnect with your true self and show up every day with spirit and presence. *You* are the only person who can change the way you move through the world. *You* are the person who has to bring your whole self and your best contributions to work every day. And *you* are the person who has to be clear about what you *actually want to experience at work* or in life.

Over the years I have worked with entrepreneurs and professionals as well as executives in large global organizations. Many of them are happy for the chance to stretch in their careers, but most of them inherit teams that seem to have lost their way in the chaos of change. So whether they're not clear about what they want to do next or how to engage those who have disconnected, they have to work on reconnecting themselves to others and the others to the work. No set of circumstances will light a spark for another human being unless that person has a reason to care or is committed to the cause, the product, the team, the company, or his or her own career.

Cheri worked as a sales rep for three years in a radio station I managed. She seemed angry over the course of a month and missed her weekly sales goals. Because we shared the sales data with our entire sales team she saw herself move to the bottom of the list of 12 sales people and started coming in later and leaving earlier, ignoring requests to attend company events. I met with her after most people had gone late one afternoon and inquired about what was happening,

"You are a really talented sales person," I told her.

"Well you are not treating me that way," Cheri explained.

Stunned, I asked, "Well, how would you like to be treated?"

She started crying. I sat still for what seemed like an eternity.

"I don't know," she finally said. "I am just miserable here."

For a minute I personalized that... but waited for the words to come.

"Cheri, what do you really want?" I asked.

"I really want to be an actress and study and perform on Broadway!"

That was unexpected and foreign to me. But it made sense. She had dressed the part of an actress. She had always had a dramatic and entertaining personality. She was big energy. I could see her there. So I asked, "Well, how can I help you realize that dream?"

That changed the conversation.

"I just need to save some money, which I had been doing until this month when my sales tanked."

So I responded with an invitation for her to determine how much she needed for a move and challenged her: "Cheri, what will it take for you to have the most amazing three months of your sales career so you can make this move before the end of the year. I will help you with a plan."

We worked her plan together. I helped with the strategy and she did the work.

I had time to find a stellar sales person and replacement.

Everyone won.

She did go to NYC. She studied with some of the best. She landed commercial work right away, both there and back home.

She satisfied that need. Cheri ended up in another career field in education, one that she loves . . . no regrets.

With a simple coaching conversation and ongoing support, Cheri was able to leap in a way that reconnected her to a longing. Consider reconnecting to your zeal by having an honest conversation with yourself.

Journal Prompts

Journaling is an honest conversation you have with yourself. It is why kids keep diaries to write their heart's desires. They are trying to discover the right language. I've found journaling is easier if you pose a question at the top of the page and write the answers that come from your heart center, at least tapping into your wisdom someplace below your neck is a good start. Breathe into your answer before you write it and then don't judge it, just scribe. You can edit later. Trust this: If you will do this one simple exercise, you will catch the wisdom that lives beyond your brain, beyond yourself, and expands your thinking and worldview so that if you need to rewrite your narrative about the career equation, it becomes an easier thing to do so.

Take the time to answer the following questions in the way that seems most appropriate to you, whether that's a traditional written answer, a diagram, or a vision board—whatever moves you!

When am I going to work at something that's big enough for my spirit?

When have I been most happy in my work?

What would I do if I had all the time in the world and knew I wouldn't fail?

What lights me up?

Where am I leading or influencing others now?

Career Investment Portfolio: Emotional, Financial, or Educational

Dan lives at the top of a Blue Ridge Mountain in North Carolina. He is retired from service in the US Navy and also a retired CEO. He lives now as an artist woodworker, carving bowls out of tree burls or hand-turning exquisite furniture. For fun - - and because he has the biggest toys and tools on the mountain including a tractor, he plows the road and driveway to our cabin and does so with great care and enjoyment. You can tell Dan lives zoetically by looking at his garden and his handicrafts. When he learned I was working on this book, he offered this wisdom:

> "I told my children the same thing I told my employees. Every job is an investment with a payoff in one of three ways: financial, educational, or emotional. If you get into a job you don't like, figure the payoff in one of these three areas, and if you can't find the gain in at least one, move on!"

Can you imagine a company of any size from a handful of employees to hundreds of thousands where every employee sees their career as an investment strategy - - truly engaged in expanding their knowledge, giving their best, learning something or landing in their right career? In this way, they are not just fulfilling job descriptions or creating products and delivering services, but wholeheartedly contributing their talents and spiritual gifts? When I say *spiritual,* I'm talking about all spiritual gifts—seeing, intuiting, serving, leading, translating, igniting others, loving, caring, and healing through words or actions. Can you imagine the extraordinary game of work you would play as part of an exceptional company of people who metaphorically hold their work in the form of the nesting bowls carved by Dan from the burled trees in our mountain? The first bowl holds the vocation. The second bowl fits inside that one and holds the career, and the third bowl holds the job. The bowls don't fit into each other if you try to stack them job first, then career and vocation. Note that your most fitting vocation is often best discovered by looking into your avocation or hobbies first. Try your hand at playing with the natural gifts you have within, then move into that as a part-time role, until you are willing to take the bigger risk and go for it.

What Would It Take to Experience a Most Extraordinary State of Being?

Play with that notion for a moment. What if your vocation led you to this team, and this company was the best place for you to express your work in a way that was completely energizing and fun? What if this was the best place on the planet for you personally to come to work? What if you couldn't wait to go play each day? What if you had to pinch yourself every morning to know you weren't dreaming?

Try raising those questions among your colleagues at the water cooler instead of complaining about the recent travel and entertainment expense cuts. Push possibility and watch transformation take place! We need all kinds of thinkers. We need people who are courageous enough to become change agents. We need people who can model hope and possibility. We need more zealots. Are you willing to join the ranks of the fully awake? Are you ready to see possibility?

It's time for your next growth spurt. It's time to reconnect and call your spirit back into your work. The world needs you. We want you to know that you are perfect for us: Your gifts and talents were packaged in just the right way for service in this stage of our evolution. We cannot stay focused on the ills of the world and live with a feeling of being out of control, without realizing that we are the only ones who can find the answers and the way back into full-fledged humanity, sharing a home. We are the purveyors of hope, and we can influence others. It will take all of us to manifest the desired changes. You are now and have always been enough to help us sort these problems out. It is time to amaze ourselves and all those who witness our work with what we do and who we become together.

You are the one we have been waiting for.

ReHumanize

Employee

I met a traveler from the corporate land
Who said: "Decaying mannequins
Spoil on their ergonomic thrones, visages
Perishing, irises now faded by aged neon
Screaming "Vacancy." Tips at eternal rest among home keys,
Tuned out, deaf to meaning, overcome by mindless noise
Their stories puddle on marble floors
Where Soul loosed its Will

And in 12-point Arial these words appear:

"My name is Employee, Creator of value,
Collector of revenue, Author of innovation
Look at Me, see Me, ye Mighty, and despair.
In conference calls and endless meetings, my
Calling misplaced. I feigned attendance while painfully
Absent. Among the fire drills it is I that became
Extinguished. Once a proud herald of the mission,
Now replaced by lifeless stretched flesh."

Greg Doherty, Change Agent

The Fourth Path Back to the Light:

ReHumanize

This fourth section of *Zombies to Zealots* is about liberation—unleashing people to stand tall as we celebrate being together here and now—at this time and space on the planet. It is what I refer to as *rehumanization,* and it is an invitation for you to become an agent of change, a revolutionary leader, and a purveyor of hope, beginning right where you are now. It is an opportunity to ignite others so they are able to wake their spirits and bring their best selves to work. What you have done for yourself, you can now guide others to do for themselves.

Rehumanizing workplaces will require that we create new ways of working. Since the beginning of time, humanity has looked up and out for answers to our big questions. Now we are sincerely looking within as well. We are going to need to reframe our approaches and behave differently, including how we lead and how we team. We will need to rethink and redefine *employee.* Whether we are the executive who leads others, the business owner, or the maintenance worker, we share this commonality: we are entering a time of integration of the known and unknown—of knowledge and discovery. Business owners of all shapes and sizes are being called on to bring a new energy to our work. We must learn to partner and team in new ways if we are going to rehumanize workplaces and reawaken the human spirit in work.

Redefining *Employee*

Every major dictionary uses the following type of definition for *employee*, which also sums up the flat and disconnected feeling that comes with being called one:

> *Employee*: Someone who is hired to work for another person, firm, or organization in exchange for a salary.

Unfortunately, a lot of people view being an employee as one step above enslavement, as if they have no choice but to show up and function in ways that diminish their spirit. The way that *employee* is commonly defined can make people feel disconnected; add the swirl of constant change that is characteristic of many organizations today and we make people feel out of control.

It's true that most organizational changes occur outside the control of those most impacted by them, leaving many asking, "What do I want now? I know it's not this. This isn't right, and I have no voice and no power in this situation." That notion led me to choose to include in this chapter the poem, titled "Employee," which was written by a change agent partner and friend of mine, Greg Doherty. A former academician and intellectual soul who has worked in business excellence and process improvement for the past four years, he aced my request to capture the feeling of most employees these days. The poem that began this section led me to write this *ReHumanize* chapter and to feature in it a story of twenty-five change agents, including the poem's author, who became catalysts of awesomeness and brought about huge results in one organization. Their story follows under "Shift 4: Become the Change Agent."

Honoring our own humanity and the humanity of those around us can be a brain squeeze. Most of us have either led or become a disengaged employee at some point in our careers, so we can relate. It is not fun or easy for the leader to manage or for people to grow beyond this situation. Yet it is possible. This process might be easier if we reframe some concepts, beginning with a deeper look at what it means to be an employee.

Given the tone of Doherty's poem and our journey together in this book, if you now believe that the word *employee* is often equated with *zombie* or that it feels less than descriptive of who you really are, then I imagine you will agree with me that it is high time we redefine the word.

Try this:

Employee:
1. A soul.
2. A human spirit at work.

That's a little different, isn't it? If we can learn to see teammates, leaders, entrepreneurs, service providers, consultants, investors, and stakeholders as souls (rather than robots, thoroughbreds, full-time employees, headcount, or workhorses), we might adapt our approaches and how we regard each other. In my first radio sales job, I once misspelled *human* as *hueman* on a copy request form for a commercial. Embarrassed by my mistake, I picked up a pencil to correct it—and then paused, as the word seemed to bounce off the page. It spoke to me. This notion of hue-man brought forth to my mind's eye the energy and color of a light-bearing being.

Seeing humans in this light offers perspective, and it also plays a part in our collective awakening. We learn to look beyond the obvious and seek to understand the energy at play in the midst of our conversations, commute, meetings, and more. Are people alive and intrigued, or are they dumbed down and disconnecting? The workplace zombies sleepwalk through their day, never considering any possibility beyond the apparent physical reality, grasping at possessions, hiding from the light. A hue-man realizes that in any situation there is much more going on than meets the eye and seeks to find more by playing with the energy and information between others and visible objects. A hue-man takes great joy in unwrapping each day as if it were a gift of discovery—something to behold, to see with new eyes or with our mind's eye, that part of us that opens to energy and to wisdom.

We might also stand a better chance of finding the chaos of change to be an incubator for creativity, innovation, and revolution if we could see that our team is made up of hue-man souls who support and sustain us through transitions, change, and even organizational restructures. In that light, these constant changes and chaos become crucibles for new beginnings on our souls' evolutionary path together.

So far, this book has been about personal transformation, which is the key to making any change stick. We can only control ourselves and our approach in any game, after all. Yet we influence others with our personal leadership and are instrumental in driving needed changes wherever we go. We are all part of teams as these are the biggest business unit that drives organizations. To change the bigger game we will need a team of like-minded partners. If we shift our worldview about what's possible, we will have a shot at changing the bigger game and winning at work.

Coaching shifts perspectives and helps people focus on the possibility of living and working wholeheartedly. Coaching as a method of development can help people frame and reframe thinking and responses moment to moment, in essence raising consciousness. Coaching doesn't take us into a state of being that is empirical or absolute, but one that is flexible and accommodating to what we hold as truth. The messages within this section were written with that frame of reference—and for your contemplation. Some of this work has been part of my own explorations. Some of this work comes from my actual experiences of delivering coaching on a scale that has created organizational shifts, and some of this work is an invitation for where we might start to drive needed changes based on where we focus our time and energy. Please read this section with these notions in mind.

It is easy to conceptualize humanity as being too large for comprehension. It may be helpful to refine how we define it:

Humanity: Who WE are and who WE are becoming *together*

We can either make the game of work about sustaining humanity on this planet and choose to be a part of the first wave of this movement, or unconsciously spin in place—zombified— waiting to see how things play out. Beginning now requires us to shift from ego concerns with "what's in this job for me" to more fully understanding who we are and who we can become together and all that that perspective makes possible—a shift in orientation from *what* we are doing to *who we are,* if you'd like the shorter version.

Dehumanization: A Brief Recap

Let's briefly review a few reasons people feel dehumanized at work:

- Chaos and speed of change are exhausting and we lose hope.
- Immediate gains in shareholder earnings are priorities considered above and before the needs of those tasked to deliver expected results.
- Preservation is valued over innovation.
- Unprepared leaders inherit seasoned teams and are unaware of those teams' capabilities and contributions.
- People feel dismissed when leaders don't listen.
- Improvement processes are prioritized over culture and people development.
- War metaphors and language—hitting the targets, crushing or killing the competition, nailing their coffins, using bullet points, gun to the head—can unconsciously frame work in violent terms.
- Employees struggle rather than play.
- Lack of communication makes progress next to impossible.
- Greed and need for speed sideline excellence.

These behaviors are as old as mankind. But they are also increasingly apparent and the default position for many cultures. If we focus on just the last point—greed—you can point to industries that have this at their core. And YOU know that greed is not a new motivation for people. Yet greed and fraud are being paraded around in headlines in a way that should give us all pause if we are to rehumanize our workplaces. Over the past few decades, a lack of integrity in the financial industry has hit the heart of our fears, forcing us to be wary and cynical about the people who manage our money. Money and what it represents is the place where we hold our hopes and most of our fears.

Dehumanization in our organizations has led many of us to develop a broader lack of trust in our society, as we've watched employees who felt they had to lie, or do something completely out of integrity, spread this viral epidemic beyond their companies and into news headlines. Our antennae are tuned to deceit, afraid of what lies beyond or behind the commercial products or services of many larger organizations.

Those who've survived many forms of standardization learned to play a different game. Replicate a standardized sales process? Check. Assess and test people daily? Check. Spoon-feed employees only what they need to know to stay in compliance with oversight agencies or global business practices?

Checkmate.

Leading a high-performing organization may require scorecards of checks and balances. I get that. In fact, I have helped create a number of those through our team-coaching processes. But leading high-performing teams also requires us to change the game of work. We must inspire others to use their executive brains

133

to design new products and services, problem solve, innovate, and act on their boldest ideas. We have to change the way we lead the people who are responsible for delivering results so they have a hand and voice in creating it.

We are now poised to rehumanize work, because we have hit a point where people are ready for liberation, are waking up to more conscious behaviors and communication, and are simply beyond ready for a change if it means they feel seen, heard, and valued.

Four Shifts for Leading and Teaming to Make Now as You Begin the Movement to Rehumanize Your Organization

Aside from redefining *employee,* which will be a big shift in our collective approach to working, there will need to be a few shifts that leaders and change agents like you can drive to get some traction in this revolutionary process.

First, a definition and context:

The word *shift* often brings to mind a shift in gears, a change that is instant and transcendent, so much so that it has a sudden and sustainable impact. Thinking about how to best explain shifts, I mentally noted just how unconscious and reactionary we are most of the time. You see this unconscious behavior in everyday interactions. Stimulus meets same responses and often reactions from same people behaving in the same ways. Trying to work through big changes is not easy if we try to do so without a wisdom guide to help us understand that we have lost something we have invested so much of ourselves in. Yet it is possible to study and coach yourself to break through illusions about how you view things and to learn to trust the realm of light and truth. That will help you take the new actions needed. We are not as a society very good at inner work and reflection. Yet, we are calling practices into our reality that allow us to focus our attention and to go within. This process is much easier if you find a creative partner, a masterful coach to work with, as your guide to inner wisdom.

In our study of archetypes with Jim Curtan, a faculty member of our coaching institute, Jim uses the learner inside each of us as a pattern of energy we have available to use for reason and discernment. It is just one of the voices or patterns of energy that roam around inside our heads. Know what I mean? Those voices that debate and compare us when we are in the car alone, and some that haunt us, have been around a long time. They are constantly battling for your attention.

Your learner is a quiet, internal voice. It doesn't shout but beckons you to pay attention to what is most right for you. Here's a method to help you hear it. Find a still point—a mental time-out place to catch and release your thoughts for about twenty minutes, with an intention to find your path within. Sitting with this quiet voice, you will notice your internal storytelling, the lies and justification you tell yourself, and the truths you are facing. You may notice how your fears surface quickly. Concerns with love, acceptance, money, stability, certainty, and wellbeing are the things that surface most immediately. Your needs for self-preservation, adventure, and social connection drive the voices that roam around in your head. This is where your learner lives. Your learner helps you clarify the choices in front of you on the basis of the truths that surface, your past experiences, and the unfolding of your desires.

Here are some mind-sets you might review to best identify what is needed around you and those you lead. The words used in the two columns that follow are clues to behaviors you may witness in those who are stuck in the daily muck and those who are in the flow of conscious and focused activity. Your mission, should you be willing to take it on, is to help others get in touch with their inner wisdom in the form of perspective from their small, inside voice or learner. To invite change is to help people who are stuck in self-destructive or zombie patterns find their way back into the light of personal empowerment and connection.

Here's some common language that can be heard in organizations—some negative, some positive—and I am offering this list to help you begin to listen for the differences.

Old Voices Mind-Set: Stuck	Learner Mind-Set: Possibility
I can't	We can
Surviving	Thriving
Drama	Possibilities
Judgmental	Acceptance
Anger	Neutrality
Sabotaging	Contributing
Needy	Whole
Lies	Truth
Assumptions	Understanding
Coping	Balancing

Should	Will
Withholding	Communicating
Victimization	Ownership
Adrenaline up and spent	Energized capacity
Fear	Love

You will find it is easier to get others to move if you move first. If you simply change your language—shifting consciously from the left column of stuck behaviors and attitudes to the right column with words focused on what you can control—you will start a movement. Someone has to be the first to take positive action. That is what a change agent does. If you lead or influence others, you can simply catch the behaviors listed in the left-hand column and become curious in how you raise questions and listen to others to help everyone shift to the right-hand column.

Following are some language samples for engaging others in a conversation for shifts:

"Mary, you appear stuck in this situation. What would it take for you to feel like you were in control and moving ahead?"

"Larry, you seem to be withholding some truth about how you really feel now. What do you want to express that really needs to be said aloud, in ways that have you feeling heard and appreciated?"

"Pat, you don't appear happy and seem to be sabotaging your current team efforts by not participating fully. It must really stink to play this small game. What's the bigger game you can imagine playing with this team without changing all the players?"

If you really want to have some fun, try sharing these Z2Z shifts with others. You go first and consider how you would "mine the gap" between the left and right columns. What behaviors, attitudes, or actions would you add or subtract to shift from one side to the other? If you complete this exercise, it will be easier for you to witness movement in others.

From Zombie	Mine the Gap	To Zealot
Naval Gazing		Stargazing
Half-Hearted		Whole-Hearted
Mindless		Mindful
Forehead Slapping		In the Flow
Competitive Advantage		Transcendent Change
Daft		Daring
Unreal (Get Real)		Surreal

These shifts take you into a deeper dialogue with people.

Next, let's explore five mind-set and behavior shifts to kick this rehumanizing movement into high gear. The word *shift* can mean a simple tweak or a giant leap in a conversation and the actions taken as a result. Either a tweak or a leap indicates a readiness to consciously choose next steps or to change perspectives. As we undertake these shifts in consciousness, we experience new and different energy in conversations and sense that others have new clarity, appreciation, and understanding.

Here are the first five shifts to explore as you take steps toward rehumanizing your workplace. Note as you read through these, that you may be closer than you think. Humanity is not lost. We are creative and have figured some stuff out. So why the arm dragging and sad faces? What if we accepted the notion that we are close to rehumanizing our workplaces? What would we need to do now to completely realize a goal of having energized people who want to partner in this endeavor?

Shift 1: TEAMING – THE SHIFT From "I, Me, Mine" to "We, We, We!"

There is a word from South African roots, *ubuntu*, that captures the essence of this shift and distinction. It is defined in *Wikipedia* as follows:

> *Ubuntu:* a <u>Nguni</u> <u>Bantu</u> term roughly translating to "human kindness." It is an idea from the region which means literally "human-ness," and is often translated as "humanity toward others," but is often used in a more philosophical sense to mean "the belief in a universal bond of sharing that connects all humanity."[7]

When I first heard this word a decade ago, I understood it to mean, "I am because we are," and that made sense to me. Said another way, "I can only be who I really am when I am a part of the bigger game everyone in my world is playing." An actor can only be an actor in the company of an audience. A teacher can only be a teacher in the company of students. I am a coach because

139

leaders need and want creative partners to challenge and guide them and their teams to achieve extraordinary things and to get better in how they relate. We get to be who we really are—our most genius selves—only in the company of those who need and want what we contribute.

Consider the world leaders who have driven the biggest changes—they have typically been one person on a big mission. Think of your favorite person to quote—is this person a poet, a musician, a spiritual guru, a world leader, or maybe a grade school teacher who spoke, wrote, or sang in a way that moved you? All of these people cared enough about those missions to step out and step up; they had an unspoken faith that what they did mattered to others.

One significant reason it is important for you to gain clarity about who you really are and what calls to you as I defined in the first sections of this book is so that you can become an expression of your most brilliant self in the work of determining who we are together. From that viewpoint, you will learn to witness those around you as your noble challengers, impatient teachers, cherished colleagues, and devoted friends; they are the loves of your life and your soul mates, even if they drive you crazy. These are the ones you have called into your life and onto your path so you can learn some stuff and grow professionally and spiritually. If you look back over the course of your life, some of the toughest and most meaningful life-changing decisions came as a result of the challenges from these people and situations.

You're not at the whim of others. You're not an out-of-control fleshy skeleton or a hollow-eyed zombie with no brain, heart, or capacity for making conscious choices. You're an active participant in your own life, whether that's succumbing to the chaos around you or rising above it.

You are brainy and creative, and when you're on the path to zealing out, you might want to consider the following shifts in the way you think about all those characters who show up on your path throwing walls, spitballs, or hurdles at you. Simple shifts in thinking can completely alter how you frame uncomfortable situations or icky challenges and can have you looking below the surface for opportunities. Here are some examples:

- *Zombie Boss*: Maybe he is your most noble challenger in disguise and there is something more for you to learn from this relationship. As you look below the surface, you may find that your zombie boss is a study in fear—like others who are frozen in space, uncertain, and lacking confidence about how to take the first steps toward change. Considering that fact changes your view and you have a different choice to make: You may decide to meet the challenge of creating a new relationship, gaining insights and some compassion in the process, or you may realize that it is time to be soulfully selfish and simply choose to move on. Just notice that you may meet that zombie boss again and again in other situations until you learn the bigger lesson you are meant to master. Maybe it means you forgive yourself and those people around you, especially this boss, when you or others tend to diminish each other. The big responsibility is that you will need to change first, so wake up and start walking toward the light!

- *Runners*: You decide to be in the experience with others instead of staying on the outside, judging, and tripping 'em up. Now's the time for you to take your talent seriously. You have come to terms with the fact that you may need to become an entrepreneur and find the courage to step out and create your own music, product, service, or big idea instead of running from one job to the next. It may be time to partner with people with similar interests. Stop running from meaningless jobs and run to your vocation.

- *Burnt-Out Superhero*: You learn to be more focused on where you place your energy and time, and you strengthen your personal foundation. You have new practices for mindfulness and find you are in better spirits as a result. You are breathing easier, appreciating all that is working in your life, and you have given yourself a break, including a vacation. That makes you more fun to be around at work and has others warming up to you, resulting in their more easily following your lead.

Get the picture?

If so, it is time to take on this view of personal leadership when you consider your part in igniting people to bring their best to your workplace. You are always influencing and leading—whether you have the title, the role, and the compensation—so why not choose to influence and lead in ways that lift your and others' spirits?

Shift 2: From Withholding to Truth Telling!

As you prepare to navigate the next phase of your work or the onslaught of constant changes you fear are lurking, you might want to contemplate how you manifest your soul's longings through declarations and moment-to-moment personal choices. That aspect of you that knows what you really want has a still and clear voice that is directly connected to the universe. That voice is the one the universe pays full attention to. The truth of who you are and what you most want resonates loud and clear, from your thought processes to how you feel deep in your gut. The universe has an umbilical cord to your heart, so when you long for something with all your heart and with clarity of mind—bam! Manifestation. What you most wanted appears in some way, even if you can't see how perfect it is at first.

Truth accelerates change! Big time!

I have now witnessed this pattern frequently through my work with executive, entrepreneurial, and organizational clients. Had I not experienced it personally, I could not have related. At some level, when you decide that you have had enough or that the work you are doing now isn't your calling, the universe, the collective consciousness, the divine consciousness, or your higher self—whatever the heck you want to call your source of power and wisdom—takes charge and moves you in the direction of your real strength, your genius, and your heart's desires. It helps you call your spirit back into your work.

Metaphorically, it's like you're sizzling in one frying pan, reluctant to move toward what you really want, and then *fhwap*, the universe slides a spatula under your bottom and flips you into a new pan, place, or situation, seeming to smile as it beckons you to get cooking with your new ideas. It also seems quite proud of Itself. "Grow fast!" it seems to say, as if bewildered by your shock. And then the Universe winks at you, "Okay, dearie, this is what you really wanted, right?"

Very few people see the part they play in the change that occurs around them. It's far easier to go zombie—to zone out, respond passively to change, or congregate around the water cooler and complain. That way you get your daily dose of sympathy by commiserating. Yet to navigate the waves of change and come out on top, I'm asking you to tap into your true potential and seize the opportunities lurking in every upheaval. You actually directly and indirectly help manifest the outcomes of each day.

Telling your truth, just saying what is true for you, is the first step. What's true for you may be that there is a need for new ways of working. It may be that you are holding on to outdated processes and products. It may be that unfair practices are causing you and your colleagues to stop short of what you would like to contribute. Whatever the truth is for you, it is time to start telling it—and not just as a complaint around the water cooler. Speak it as a bold request for those who can hear it and drive the change. Take your requests to the highest order of leadership and watch what happens. At some level, conscious or not, they are dying to know what you think, feel, and know!

So what does *fhwapping* and truth telling have to do with rehumanizing work, zombies, and zealots? Truth telling is the key to the kingdom. Truth telling is, in fact, how we start to rehumanize our cultures. Truth telling is also contagious and when you operate out of an authentic place, you give others the courage to do the same. And being authentic = being human. Voila!

But who takes the first step? If you are a leader, definitely YOU. If you are not in a leadership position but are courageous, definitely you.

Truth telling is not so easy, given how much time our society has spent processing it out of us. The process of truth telling starts like this. First, drop your thoughts into a new place... out of your head or thinking center and into your heart center. What are you feeling right now? State that, or write it down. Keep asking yourself what's the truth behind what I am feeling until you get to the space of recognizing it as the truth.

For example, "I am feeling so uncertain about what to do next. I will just keep my mouth shut and stay out of the way until the company is ready to say what is really going on."

What's the truth behind what I am feeling? "I am scared that I will be part of the next round of cuts or be displaced from my job and my team."

What's the truth about that? "If I lose my job, I may not be able to easily replace the income with another meaningful role. I haven't had to interview in a long time. I wonder if I am employable. I may lose my partner as well. She or he depends on me for so much, and our relationship has been a little rocky lately given all my travel."

Now you are at the truth of the matter.

And given you are a brilliant problem solver, you can probably see the first thing to do is to start preparing. First, manage the details of your basecamp: Connect and have that honest conversation with your partner. Focus on your intention or desired outcome. Second, dust off your resumé and look at everything you have accomplished in the past two years. Add those things. Any course for leadership development? Any technology update? New competencies?

Then elevate the truth you see impacting you and others. Request that the leaders around you share what they can share, list what they can't, and get real with their own concerns. Just start the dialogue. Listen to those above you. What resonates? What doesn't? What don't you want to hear that you now know?

What would it take for everyone to feel like they were being treated like souls at work? How can you become curious enough about that to start that dialogue with those who can do something about it?

Shift 3: Zealot Leader – Become the Liberator

> ***The Zealot Leader***: **A zealous and courageous leader who uses her or his influence, intuitive wisdom, and passion to catalyze awesomeness, conveying viral enthusiasm while unleashing the real potential of their teams.**

Liberators not only see the brilliant souls trapped in the zombie employees who've numbed out, but they can also become a part of their rescue team and champions. A rebel pushes against convention. A liberator seizes and champions an ideal or idea. Liberators are activist leaders who search for and infuse cultures with positive momentum. A liberator first sets him/herself free, as we have outlined in the first sections of this book, and then they set others free. They are not truly free until they have retrieved the others who are still in captivity. They know that the revolution involved in this liberation is not just a personal voyage, but bigger than any one person. They believe that together, we can cultivate positivity and possibilities.

Anne as Change Agent and Zealot Leader

You read Anne's story in the introduction about how she learned to work for what she really wanted. Fast forward a few decades to the time when Anne hired me as her coach as she had just been promoted from district sales manager into a regional vice president role and wanted some help navigating the inherent dynamics in the company and for her team, as she was also being considered for even more demanding roles and responsibilities.

Anne instinctively knew how to support the sales stars on her team. When I interviewed each of her team members to gain insights into how Anne was doing in this new position, it was clear that they regarded her with a degree of adoration, bordering on hero worship. They made almost no suggestions for her to change or become more effective; in fact, they all wanted to see her run the company. The concern they voiced was this, "Anne works so tirelessly and has such high expectations of herself, we are afraid she may expect the same of us." They were committed to Anne but at the same time worried about keeping her pace.

So when I gave her their feedback in a theme report, I could see the concern in Anne's eyes and hear it in her voice. While Anne admitted that she worked a lot of hours, she didn't have the same expectation of others. Based on the lessons from her early years, she felt she had to hustle and work harder than others to ultimately reach the goal of running the company. However, she was quite troubled by the potential negative impact she could be having on people and their families. This realization put Anne in a reflective state to examine the impact of her work habits on her own young family as well. She made new agreements with her family and now laughs about the fact that her husband kept her honest by padlocking the French doors to her home office after she worked late on a Friday night and she could only stand and peer through the glass Saturday morning as monthly financial reports rolled off the fax machine.

Anne says this time was a "pivot point" for how she integrated her life and work, as well as coached others to live life and work fully engaged. She realized by taking time out to recharge and engage fully with her family and friends, she became a better leader, wife, mother, and friend. She also realized that it opened a vast energy source that enabled her to give even more to her people and work. It was then that she realized she had the motivation and courage to pursue a bigger role in the company and even declare her ultimate goal.

"I want to run the company one day," Anne offered quietly and deliberately during one of our coaching sessions, as if saying this out loud would jinx the possibility.

"So, where do you want to start preparing for that role?" I asked.

Anne explained that the company wanted her to move into a new marketing position. Some of the senior leaders wanted her to "broaden her experience," and she was toying with that possibility. But as I watched her describe the new opportunity, I noticed her obvious change in energy. "When you talk about this role, you sound like a cat spitting out a hairball!" I exclaimed. Both of us burst into laughter. The fact was, Anne didn't want to go into marketing. It wasn't what called her. The vice president of sales training role was opening up, and that was the position she wanted.

Anne felt she would have real impact there and be able to make a contribution. The position fit her skill set. Yet, when Anne grew more comfortable with me in our coaching sessions, she acknowledged that she was an introvert and had some real fears about speaking up in meetings with senior leaders and voicing her opinion. In response, I encouraged her to tap into her belief in the team and the role she should play in contributing to the performance of the business. I challenged Anne to remember what she most wanted to be known for, making a difference in people lives, and enabling them to be their best self, and to find and feel her feet in those difficult moments (grounding to her energy source—an old actor's trick for handling nervous energy). We retrained Anne's inner rebel to use her "I can do it!" energy and hustle in a new way. We enabled her to convince others they were enough and to contribute their best.

She landed the new position as the VP of Sales Training. Even better, she also found her voice as she kept this simple notion in mind: She was now the spokesperson for each of those people in the field who loved her. Anne became a strong advocate for women in her company, championing an accelerated women's development program to help other women find their voice and create a career path. Now, almost a decade after its launch—and long since its original sponsors, including Anne, have moved on in their careers—this program continues as a best practice for engaging and promoting women in that company.

As Anne's career opportunities have taken her to new places, she has continued to carry a light for others and to ignite their inner sparks. She learned to trust that she *is* enough and that others are enough, even if they need to find other roles to be more fulfilled. As her story continues to unfold, she maintains energizing others as one of her primary responsibilities as a leader. She achieved her goal of running international companies, and she has grown her reach as a world-class leader. It is an honor to have been a part of her journey, and I will continuously cheer her, this introverted, powerhouse, and revolutionary zealot leader as she tackles new frontiers!

Revolutionary leaders find ways to showcase what's working and add a spark of light or inspiration to their communication. They tell the truth, especially about the things that are changing. Their passion, transparency, and sense of purpose are wholeheartedly contagious. They become the liberators for others who are in the same places they were once.

I also want to acknowledge right about now that some of you may be growing weary of the notion that people could actually be fired up and zeal filled every day. Therefore, part of this next shift holds nuts-and-bolts game plans for those who cannot stomach the idea of dancing on the lawn with exuberant colleagues or even muster the energy to think about sustaining that type of enthusiasm. There are things you can do to become an agent of change right where you are, right now. It will require personal growth from you, in the form of an investment of time, energy, and attention into developing yourself into a new type of leader.

Shift 4: Becoming the Change Agent

As Ghandi said, "Be the Change you wish to see in the world." I use that quote to inspire my next question: "How do you Become the Change you wish to see at work?" If you want to change the nature of an element in a scientific experiment, you typically need heat and a chemical catalyst—in other words, a change agent. The same thing is true in organizations and societies. If you genuinely want to catalyze change and do so in an impactful way, especially in moving the majority of your employee base from dispirited or just fine to engaged, inspired, and exuberant culture champions, you are going to need to ignite them by bringing some heat or demonstrating a significant contrast in your approach to changing leadership and the process.

Bringing heat means that you are ready to invest in a scientific experiment that has proof of concept. It means you are willing to challenge your organization to create a dynamic shift in the methods you use to conduct business, for both people and processes. It means you are able to have emotion-filled conversations and get into the humanity of people so they feel safe to explore and deconstruct what isn't working so that you may create space for growth.

I've dedicated this book to the change agents—all culture champions and leaders—that I've been privileged to teach and coach in several organizations. We have designed change programs based on a simple conversational coaching model that shifts and lifts these organizational cultures. So what exactly is a change agent?

> *Change agent*: A culture champion who sees the best in others and helps to unleash possibility every day.

In small companies, this is the person who sees the needed changes and helps the owner or leader find ways to drive those changes by supporting each soul to give their best efforts. In that way they help to create the culture they want to experience.

In a large organization the change agent is a soul who represents the face and the voice of his or her colleagues to create a transparent communication loop to senior-level leaders and back to the front line in two ways. First, the change agent listens fully to the organization, and second, the change-agent coaches leaders to take actions that accelerate needed changes to engage people to give discretionary effort. In the words of someone who took on this role in a large organization for two years:

> My role as a change agent is to act as a catalyst to build capabilities that will put the organization in a position to change to meet the needs of a rapidly shifting business and customer landscape. The leadership who sanctioned the placement of change agents understood that if we work to change processes, [adapt] business approaches, and foster innovation without undertaking significant cultural change, we would be setting the organization

up for frustration. As change agents, our first order of business was to shift the water cooler dialogue from "what is wrong" to "what is possible?"

—Doug Buriani, Change Agent and Sales Leader

You might not yet think of yourself as a change agent, given that most of you haven't had that title or have not yet been introduced to this as a professional role. Yet, if you have cared deeply about people, especially your teammates and the teams you lead now; if you have listened deeply to the souls around you; and if you have risked sharing your truth when you felt it could make a difference, then you are already on the path.

When we asked "Employee" poet Greg and his colleagues to recast their roles from front-line leaders or senior sales reps to change agents and declare their first 120-day mission, they stated one clear and compelling goal: "Change the water cooler conversation from 'I can't' to 'we can!'"

These change agents participated in a two-year project that promised investment in their professional development but no guarantee that any of them would have jobs in the company to return to after this two-year change initiative was complete, so signing up for the role was a big risk. Yet, they were willing to represent their friends and colleagues—to, in essence, reflect the heart of the company—even if doing so placed their own tenure on the line. They had experienced being surrounded by disengaged friends and coworkers, and they cared deeply about bringing a new level of energy, hope, and—dare I say it—zeal to their teams.

A Change Agent's Secret Advantage
is a Coaching Conversation

> *Coaching is a creative partnership based in thought-provoking dialogue that engages people to take action for meaningful work and life.*

When I asked the change agents to help us describe their role and the change leadership process we engaged them to drive, Craig Flanagan, the associate vice president of business excellence and the change agent team leader, replied:

> "After accepting the challenge of positively impacting our company's culture, I started down a path that I knew needed to be blazed but [that I] didn't quite know how to navigate. The Pyramid Resource Group coaches had a framework of a plan from which we created a journey map. They taught me and my team the necessary coaching and change leadership skills to challenge our organization to speak the truth and set people free to become their best selves. It was a difficult, rewarding, frustrating, and fun journey that had a positive impact on employee engagement and, most importantly, on many teams and individuals across the organization.
>
> Many people discovered a renewed passion for their work or a new passion for something they didn't even know was possible. What I am most proud of is the work of our group of Change Agents, I was honored to lead. They put

their own needs aside and poured their hearts and souls into making positive changes for their fellow employees. Their skill level, dedication, and perseverance were the keys to our success and the spark that ignited the dramatic change.

I am thankful for the personal and professional growth I've experienced through this journey and I continue to see the impact of our work on teams and individuals across the organization. This was the most rewarding two years of my career and I will forever be a better husband, father, friend, and leader because of it."

For the change agents that Craig led, the coaching role wasn't just a time-out or a break from the traditional roles they had played; it was a calling to more symbolic work on their career journey and to a way of being that meant a life change. After our work together, they could never go back to their old ways of working or living again. The shifts they made were permanent, and they modeled change and created possibility for others around them as Craig noted above —especially in the feedback they gave to more senior leaders. They learned to engage others in deep inquiries and conversations that catalyzed better ways of working together. At first they followed our lead, but within a few months, they were co-creators and took the lead themselves, which was our desired outcome.

Lifting Employee Engagement by 30 Points in Less than a Year

Curious about the results that occurred from the two-year change-agent initiative? The work of these change agents went far beyond coaching the regional leaders and teams to change the water cooler dialogue to "we can!" At the end of their first year, their coaching approach had boosted employee satisfaction and engagement in significant ways. Working together with the company's top leadership to problem solve and address leadership challenges, these change agents created a new narrative around the company that lifted employee engagement from 61.4 percent to 90.4 percent in an accelerated way.

We launched a survey through Haysmar, Inc., with research partner, Lynn Hays. She found that when it came to people and processes, the people piece was the larger part of the equation and that people articulated what they were feeling, not what they were thinking. These comments are from her report:

1) Employees felt weary, drained of energy, and like they lacked direction or a sense of power because of company mergers, ongoing restructuring, and efforts to integrate and streamline cultures and processes.

2) The company used a calibrated performance management system that was incorrectly perceived by employees to be part of the downsizing. The unintended consequence was that it exacerbated the underlying fear of job loss.

3) Cost containment measures, necessary but painful, were implemented and created further frustration among employees.

Do any of these themes sound familiar? Maybe like a global epidemic? As is often the case with initial surveys in a changing environment, once employees felt confident that they wouldn't be harmed by their candor, the floodgates opened. In this case, 1,660 of the 1,901 respondents used the unlimited comment space, which translated into more than one hundred pages of often emotionally charged appeals for change. Comments are a rich source of candid insights, and providing them gives employees a sense of catharsis by allowing them to verbalize their suggestions and aspirations for the company.

Once the themes were understood by leaders, quick and visible actions were taken in response, demonstrating to employees that their voices were being heard and heeded. Although solutions to the broader issues were being digested and explored, some simple wins helped to get employees' attention, such as relaxed meeting attire, the reintroduction of team-building activities, and increased opportunities to telecommute. These quick fixes were followed by tangible process improvements, such as accelerating the deployment of new technology and computers to the field professionals. Other improvements, such as reducing the number of decision layers and revising a ride-along system for field sales, helped to further show employees that they were valued and respected. This supplemented the increase in leader communications, improving transparency and trust in leadership. Though all of the leadership competencies measured by the company had significant increases in team and self-reporting, the most impactful improvement was that leadership inspired an environment of openness and trust—an increase from 43.9 percent to 87.0 percent, a total rise of 43.1 percentage points in one year. Excitingly, the results of the follow-up survey after the first year of our work together showed that significant improvements in company culture and core competencies were universal and accomplished in a remarkably short time.

Teaming

Change is difficult, and working with many models and processes takes time and can be daunting. What needed to change first for the change agents was how people listened to and heard each other. They were lucky to have senior leader champions helping to drive the initiative so there was freedom of movement, internal communication plans, and an investment of capital that supported their efforts. This was the ideal approach that became a research project for us all. It is in the spirit of what we learned that I offer a simple, three-step, cultural game-changing plan below as a roadmap to start the process of *rehumanizing* your company, regardless of the size or number of employees. Just realize that this case study was of a larger company, but that the principles and process can apply for most any size company.

Also, note that this is just a pattern for starting the conversation. Once you start this process, you may be called on to team with others in new ways to help change the game.

Are you ready?

Prep

If you are in the position to do so, name a group of change agents to represent divisions or regions of your workforce. Or if you are done with all of the doom and despair around you and find yourself in a small company, appoint yourself a change agent and start a zealot circle. A zealot circle can be a group of folks who have a covert or stated mission: to become the zombie rescue team and unleash the potential of the entire group of souls who work together in your company. This can be a job-plus role, or you may make this a covert operation with an intention to drive change or the needed shifts in your organization from wherever it is now to where you believe and hope it can be.

Before you take the next three steps, please take a few minutes to reflect and consider whether you are ready to open conversations with people so you can understand their pain and desires. If you feel you are ready to start a zealot movement but know in your gut that your work teams are in toxic places and you are not fully equipped, I recommend that you find help in your leadership team, your human resources team, or your organizational development professionals. Most leaders and human resources professionals are more than ready to change the dialogue and would love the added hands and hearts of a change agent or a team of zealots to address the zombie outbreak and accelerate needed changes. An alternative that I recommend is to find a qualified team coach to help you prepare and drive the process.

You are about to help unleash potential, but you are also going to release some raw emotion and venting when you awaken those frozen-in-place, knuckle-dragging souls posing as zombies. You will want to know that you, too, have support when you hear what people need to say. You are going to feel some of the same things others feel, so you will want to intentionally detach your story from those told by others. Put your own complaints on ice for a while. Write them in a journal and close it up so you can fully hear both what people are really saying and then what they want, which is information usually tucked underneath what they are saying. Remember that it is difficult to articulate the tough stuff or take responsibility for moving others out of toxic conversations, so be patient and allow some silence in the spaces.

If you have any questions about your readiness, start your zealot movement as a book club or zealot zone and meet twice a month with six to twelve others who are ready to become a part of the rescue team. If you own the business, you are the first in line on the journey to becoming a zealot. So you can follow the three steps below with a goal of bringing your own team to life.

Game Changers: Three Steps for Changing the Game of Work

First Step: Listen!

Go out and listen to the heartbeat and soul of your organization with the intention of discovering the top four or five themes of things that need to be addressed for the company to move from surviving to thriving. Your role as a listener will be to facilitate dialogue and understanding by getting people to talk openly. Listening is hard work that requires you to suspend judgment. According to my scientist husband, who has done a lot of work and research around listening to teach a course on that topic, the average person speaks at a rate of about 125 words per minute, yet that same person can listen to and process about 700–800 words or sound bytes per minute, so there is a big gap between our speaking speed and our mental capacity for hearing each other. That means that as a listener, you will have all sorts of time to check out, relate the stories you hear to a time when you experienced the same thing, make a mental grocery list, or whatever else you do mentally when you are functioning on autopilot. You need to notice if you tend to prepare to speak instead of truly hearing what others say and fight that tendency. Observe yourself for a day or so in your typical interactions and determine whether you can just be present with people and listen to them fully without problem solving or sharing your own story. If so, proceed! If not, you might benefit from taking a leadership coaching course or at least a listening skills course to prepare.

Once you feel prepared, conduct your listening sessions. Determine which teams you will support and how broadly you can drive a change initiative. You may only need work with one or two teams if you are a solo act or more if you are driving a larger initiative and have leadership sponsors. Conduct the listening sessions with employees seated in a circle. Plan on two to three hours for each group, depending on the number of people. Everyone needs time to fully download what they are feeling and will want to communicate a lot of information about what needs to change if you ask the right questions.

Have some exercises available to start the conversation just in case the list of questions fails to get people to speak their minds. These can be simple exercises, such as plotting where people land on the Zombie to Zealot Workplace Energy curve.

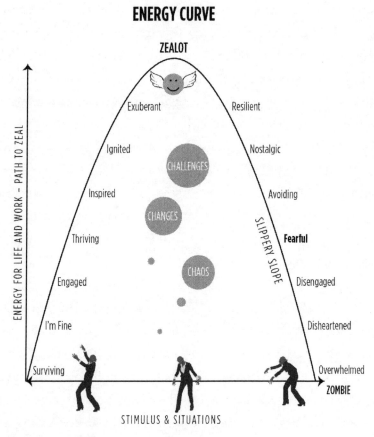

Figure 3. Energy Curve Revisited

Doing this simple exercise will help create some common language so people can clearly express their emotions and what they are experiencing. You don't need to be an expert—just be a participant. Let others know you have a commitment to help the organization hear what is needed now for everyone to fully engage. You want people to give equal weight and time to expressing both how they feel and what they think. In fact, getting emotions out first will allow more creative conversations, but be prepared to catch all sorts of venting. Once people start telling their truth, the floodgates will open. You will need to learn the difference between talking about change and driving it. These contrasts revise emotionally charged water cooler conversations and enable souls to shift their points of view from old ways of working to new ways of thinking. Change begins here. When we articulate our fears, our beautiful problem-solving minds take over to help us find solutions.

Second Step: Hear and Acknowledge!

Many issues will pop up that you will want to capture and feed back to those who share with you. Ask people, "Did I get this right? Are these the top issues and problems you believe need to be addressed for us to grow together?" Your challenge will be to identify and catalogue the information you gather in a way that will contribute to an action plan, achieve quick fixes for the easier problems, and acknowledge issues that will take longer to address. These themes can be presented to the individual division leaders and addressed by the most senior leaders in virtual town hall meetings and in leadership workshops. You want the leaders to agree that they will actually take decisive actions to make at least one or two changes now to gain trust and get people moving up the energy continuum to start zealously contributing again.

Third Step: Coaching for Change

When we train change agents, we focus on having them become completely present with people: to see others, to hear them, to hold their ideas and concerns, and to help them see hope. Hope is the ignition needed to have people move past inertia and participate. Practicing presence requires you suspend your judgments, remove yourself from the center of dramas, and shift to being a committed observer and connector. Listening, questioning, and offering perspective to shift how people see their current situations composes the basic toolbox of a change agent.

The bottom line message is that to be a change agent, you have to change first. You have to accept or try new and different approaches to accelerating change for others, but first model what you want to see and hear. People are complaining around you? Be the first to stop complaining. People are withholding the truth they see or their ability to over deliver a goal? Be the first to speak your own truth and over deliver a result. If you've never worked with a coach, this is a good time to find a certified and qualified business coach who can help you determine how to best navigate the changes you will take on. You will also be using coaching skills to facilitate conversations, so learning those through participation in a robust coaching program or coaching school is also an important step to consider.

The change agents we train in change leadership and coaching skills leave the first intensive workshops having made some significant changes in their worldviews but not fully trusting that what they have signed up for will really work. The organizational change they are about to help drive often feels way too big. Yet the process works; it just does. People are waiting—no, they're dying—to have real conversations and are beyond ready to share what they are thinking with someone who will just hear them and honor that the way they feel is real and normal. Purging the drama helps people get over themselves and move from fear-based conversation to more fearless ways of being, especially in how they communicate with each other. It just requires a kick-start and some practice.

Note: In the process of this type of change you may say something that doesn't land well. If you mess things up, apologize and ask what people need from you to clean up any misunderstanding. Keep going. Keep learning and explaining what you learned in the process. Conversational fearlessness lifts organizations. And it has to start somewhere—so you are the one to drive it now. This is your opportunity to take the lead in new ways. The thing about the laws of energy, especially the law of attraction, at play in this type of culture-changing game is that presence invites presence. Love begets love. Passion makes room for passion. Exuberance inspires more exuberance! Everything seems possible and the extraordinary feels within reach. You experience a hum of activity that even outsiders notice and warm up to. All of this is possible when you just take the leap of faith to get moving. Again, you will need to demonstrate or model those things first.

Change the Game, Change the Culture!

Cultivating trust in the leadership and in the team or company is the biggest game changer for rehumanizing work! Change agents rebuild trust in leadership, and that is the biggest challenge for most organizations. So how do you build trust in any organization?

Listen + Truth + Responsiveness = Trust

Simply, act on what you can change now.

Formulate a plan with those most impacted and bring them along in the decisions to make the needed changes that take longer. It's simple, but not easy. You have to do the work and stay committed to the best solutions, not the most immediate answers. Again… people can give up their position or need to be right if they know you are working together to do what's right for the greater good.

What to Watch Out for?

Any time there is a significant need for zombie rescue team – culture change - there are some toxic removal steps needed to insure the safety and sustainability for those rescued.

Here are the top 3 challenges that can sabotage change agent efforts and a place to start to handle these challenges:

1. Zombie Apathy and Feet Dragging Opposition – it can take a while to move Zombies into the light, so start with those who are most ready to change and highlight or celebrate the things they do to take charge of the changes you seek to implement. Don't lose heart, or brains or your guts – courage – during the process. Stay the course.

2. Zealot Leader and Champion exits company, leaving you in a lurch. If you lose your sponsor, don't lose your mission. Bring as many leaders as possible into the dialogue for positive change and create momentum as you highlight how they champion and rescue their teams from the chaos surrounding you now. Continue to create zealot enthusiasm one person, one team at a time.

3. Failure to put a structured rescue plan in place and then to evolve as you work through it – Work on creating a Journey Map with structures built into your process that can be easily replicable by every leader. Listening circle sessions can be conducted at every level – determine how you will use the themes derived from those – by highlighting the top three actions and then take those in a visible way so everyone knows you are committed to the rescue. Bring teams along with you ... learn a team leadership model for coaching– having leaders learn core coaching skills is critical to keep a culture of curiosity alive and for people to feel free to approach leaders at every level. Team coaching in the form of Team

Advantage™ accelerates ownership as people find their way to a common cause and communication platform in ways that keep key employees from the slippery slope of disheartenment.

There are real risks to becoming part of a Zombie Rescue Team and Change Agent. When you shine light into dark spaces as part of a rescue team, you get one of two reactions. People either open their arms to fully embrace you and the changes you are driving ("YAY, FINALLY SOMEONE GETS IT!") or they turn from the light and hide their eyes, at least in the short term ("Go away—who do you think you are?")

And yet, if you are a change agent, you will never leave the tools behind. You take those into your next roles. So in the case of the change agents, the original goal was to launch a two-year program *and* to train a group of people who would go back into new roles at the end of that period with new skills. In that frame, this was a covert operation of reawakening the change leader and inserting them back into management and director positions with newly acquired skills. In this way, it was sustainable.

Another challenge is that not everyone is up for an invasion of enthusiasts. Containing that level of energy and creativity requires leaders to develop a new capacity for their work. If you take on this role, you will need to do some inner work to become great with people, to develop others, and to detach from some of the beliefs about how things should be done. You will need to be clear about who you are becoming and who you are for others, in service to the larger organization and the communities it serves.

You will need to understand that you are a soul, finding light in other souls.

Meeting people in their current state—whether zombie or zealot—requires you to consider the current culture, and how to help other people determine where to start to make changes.

The really cool thing about becoming a change agent is this: you become a soul who truly cares about new ways of leading and you will lead change that others welcome. So whatever the investment in this, you have changed a culture. Others cannot go back to old ways of working when they reawaken and remember who they are.

As one sales director and forever change agent wrote recently when I asked if he was in his happy place,

> "To say I am in my happy place may be an understatement. I am now a Director. I have reshaped a *very* successful team as we launch new products using an 'open door' policy within all levels in my organization. Had I not been a change agent, I would have tried to solve *every* issue in the world. Now with the capabilities I have, I have worked to empower people to own their business, create their own solutions, and be happy being 'uncomfortable.' You and your team made a *huge* impact on me in only 10 months in the role, and now I am where I need to be—in front of 115 employees, leading and sharing visions of greatness."

Sustaining the types of shifts I recommend is challenging in a dynamic business, but sustaining changes is not impossible.

We must be willing to shift personally, so that we grow more comfortable with the discomfort of change if we are going to stay on top of the Energy Curve and stay more zealot than zombie.

A Salute to Change Agents

Shifting from disengaged employee to change agent or culture champion wouldn't be complete if I didn't offer this salute for those who have taken on this role in ways that elevated my own game. I am in awe of the change agents we've met over the past few years—the men and women my team has been privileged to call partners and to coach and guide in several companies. There are also change agents among you, the readers, who have followed your own inner voice of wisdom and have lit the way for you and others, zealously taking the lead to create great companies long before my team came on the scene.

So here's a salute to all those who have risked becoming a zealot for greatness and a catalyst of awesomeness, wherever you are.

Dear Catalysts of Awesomeness!

You are revolutionary leaders who unleash and free people to play, to stop struggling, and to reignite their spirits.

You give voice to so many who have lost their own, and you have been vulnerable in ways most people can only philosophize about in leadership conversations.

Your conversations heal the pain around you.

You celebrate people who are longing for recognition, applauding the successes of those who are ready to reawaken, remember, and reconnect.

You become a leader others willingly follow as you make your way back into the folds of your organization.

Because of your fearlessness, those who could have been lost are reawakened and come to life more fully in their work. You realize that coming to life at work translates not just to them but to their families too—so you are changing lives for the better with every listening or coaching session. Even if you leave the company, the position, or the team, you have unleashed souls and given them hope that they can win.

You are the divine spark—the change angel who lovingly guides dull-eyed zombies back to the path for their most brilliant contribution. The leaders you support have also been activated and are now illuminating the path for others.

My colleagues and I are better for knowing you, for guiding you, and for following your lead.

You are the original catalysts of awesomeness and excellence.

And to you, the reader: You are now knighted a change agent as well. If you did nothing other than read this book and make one small change to shift your thinking to possibility rather than ranting about changes or challenges you encounter then you have become a part of this movement. Keep going!

The Invitation

Humanity is an evolutionary, creative species. Regardless of how we landed on this planet, we are made up of the stuff of earth, animated by a nature beyond the dust and water, the minerals and the organs. We have become a species of unconscious caretakers and our own worst enemies. Yet, we are also our only hope, and through our awakenings and our learning, we have collectively sorted some things out. During our time here, we have learned to team, even if we are a bit wobbly in our attempt. We have asked bigger questions and conducted mind-blowing research about what else is possible. We have within us the answers we all need for not just surviving but for thriving as citizens of the larger universe.

Can we begin now to rehumanize our workplaces, to hear people, to give witness to the truths that we have buried about so many things, to sustain life on this treasure of a planet? This could be the best time to be alive. We can now see our way clear to carve a new pathway out of this current deconstruction and the darkness we are experiencing, and into an era of light and love. We only need to look up and out, and to search deep within to find the pathways to the peaceful place we all long to find.

This book acknowledges a truth that you already know: You have the potential to be wholly aligned in heart, mind, and spirit wherever you choose to play. You may have felt this alignment click into place in the short time we have spent together in these pages, or you may have brought full alignment into your reading, searching for someone who could just get who you are. Together we are growing; we are engaging others in a new dialogue to raise consciousness and lead in new ways.

This book is not really ending, but beginning a conversation to remind us that we came here to play a game together; the energy of possibility to be of great service or to have a ton of fun has lived within each of us since we were born. Now that it has been reignited, what will you do with it? This choice is entirely yours.

What small spark of your own talent are you ready to share with your team, your organization, and the world? What crazy, big idea are you ready to give birth to now? Is there a meaningful entrepreneurial venture waiting to be nurtured by your beautiful mind, your capable hands, and your soaring spirit?

Share your energy for life… your enthusiasm, your zeal in the way that works best for you. Keep your big boss suit on if you need to stay buttoned-up to be taken seriously, or put on your overalls and smock and get ready to plant and paint.

It is time—beyond time—to let the real you shine through. We do not need to go through an apocalypse to realize our evolution and understand why we are here. We do need to fear another army of dazed faces, knuckle draggers, and outstretched arms whose job it is to keep us in small, dark places, hiding our faces from the light. Our workplaces, our neighborhoods, our communities, and our planet need us!

When we fully reawaken and remember who we truly are, we can no longer sleepwalk. We cannot live or work unconsciously. When you change inside out, you are forever changed.

Remember: you cannot put a butterfly back into a chrysalis. Together, we have started a movement to rehumanize work *NOW.*

I can't wait to see what we do next!
We are the ones we've been waiting for!

A Soulful Invitation

Born of Earth and Water
Animated by Breath and Spirit
WE are humanity.
Vibrations from hearts and minds
Float on waves of energetic frequencies
Winding through an expanding Universe
Connecting us all to the great I AM
Calling us back and forth
Through a veil of light
Opening to us now as we seek the truth
Discoveries reveal what is and has been
and shall be—already there
In this place of mysteries.
We are given life in language:
"Words made flesh,"
Mere expressions of a larger blueprint.
Now in the state of messy chaos, breaking ground,
We descend to a playing field for spiritual evolution.
We ascend now to call forth all Humanity.
Master Creators,
We work together to reawaken the torch bearers now
Not to merely survive, we are preparing to thrive
As citizens of a vast and expanding *universe*
That winks to us now
Inviting us to remember and reconnect.
I am here, WE are here, with deep gratitude and awe
For all that WE are and can become
Together.

Darelyn 'DJ' Mitsch
March 2016

Zombie Rescue Team Toolkit

You and your colleagues may download the complimentary Zombie Rescue Team Tool Kit by visiting our author's page at www.ZombiesToZealots.com. This full kit is chock full of a variety of exercises for reflection such as the Energy for Work Grid, the Life Force and Energy Wheel (shown below), the Soulful Goals™ Exercise, and the Leadership Quest Exercise.

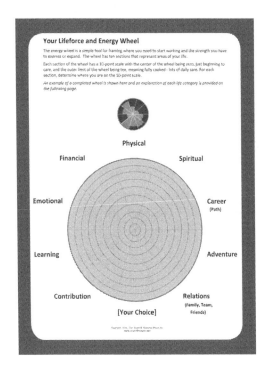

The Energy Wheel Explained

There are ten sections of the energy wheel. Key words related to each section are provided below to help you assess your personal rating in each category.

PHYSICAL

Overall physical health, right foods & eating habits, optimal weight, regular exercise, up-to-date physical exams, vaccinations, dress, energy level, hygiene, sleep patterns.

SPIRITUAL

Time for introspection, reflection, meditation, connection with a higher power, contemplative reading and/or writing a still point in your day to breathe in beauty and connect to nature.

CAREER

Satisfaction level, alignment with skills and talents, alignment with values, challenged and motivated, working with people with integrity, growth opportunities.

ADVENTURE

Travel, excitement, new challenges and events planned to stretch your imagination and experience the world.

RELATIONSHIPS

Adequate time, home base comfortable, vacations planned, open relationships, regular communication with parents, siblings and children, minimal conflict, ease of resolution. Strong network of friends, connected with community, source of fun and support.

BLANK

Is there something important to you that is not included in the categories above? Use this section of the wheel to evaluate that aspect of your life.

CONTRIBUTION

Serving your community, the world around you, volunteer work, contributions to charitable causes, making a difference through time and/or money.

LEARNING

Learning new things constantly, continuing education and training, challenging reading, skills development. Have a vehicle for growth, a field of study that supports mastery in an area of interest.

MOTIONAL

Have a lot of love in your life. Access a range of emotions and articulate those in a neutral way. Feel supported.

FINANCIAL

Debt minimized or absent, reserve funds, retirement planning, credit secure, financial advisor in place, accounts balanced, bills paid on time.

Figure 4. Your Life Force and Energy Wheel

Recommended Reading List

While I always have a long list of books to read, I've curated seven below, which I believe will contribute to the work you will do as prescribed in the Zombie Rescue Guide.

We Are the Ones We Have Been Waiting For by **Alice Walker** (New York: New Press, 2006)
This book includes the poem "Call Your Spirit Back." I have loved Alice Walker's books for many years and you will find soul food within them to prompt your thinking. You may find this one to be especially fitting as you explore the quintessential questions about your purpose and how to express it.

Sacred Contracts, Awakening Your Divine Potential by **Caroline Myss** (New York: Three Rivers Press, 2002-2003)
Reading this yummy book from bestselling author Carolyn Myss is like eating a box of the finest handmade dark chocolate on the planet. You will want to savor every little bite. She must channel much of the information in that it comes through her hand so clearly. This rich content will stop you in your tracks and have you more clearly answering the quintessential questions, "Why am I here?" and," Who am I really?"

179

***Daring Greatly* by Dr. Brene Brown** (New York: Avery/ Penguin, 2015)

Brene Brown speaks to the heart of vulnerability and how to take a leap of faith—trusting that we are always who we *think we are.* Time to change your thinking? Pick this one up and keep a highlighter handy!

Got Your Attention, POP! And Tongue Fu, and a host of other books, by Sam Horn (Best Selling Author and TED speaker)

Sitting in a circle of authors at Sam's recent writers retreat, I presented my research laden manuscript idea to 15 other amazing people, with a young attorney next to me who said, drop the manuscript, and Sam asked, "What do you do for others?" To which I replied, "I bring them back to life at work." "Because," she pried. "Because they have become zombies." "And when they work with you they become?" she continued. "Zealots!" I exclaimed. "Then you have the name of your book!" And so it was born… a whole new and better idea. Sam is indeed the intrigue expert and a world class speaker and coach. Read everything she writes!

***The 7 Habits of Highly Effective People: Powerful Lessons in Personal Change* by Stephen R. Covey** (New York, Simon and Schuster, 2013)

7 Habits is a personal leadership standard and thought provoking book that calls your attention to what matters most in your life.

The Discomfort Zone: How Leaders Turn Difficult Conversations into Breakthroughs by my colleague, Marcia Reynolds, PsyD. Building on our collective coaching models for conversations - - some we teach in our coaching program - - and her expert work around emotional intelligence and neuro-science, Marcia's books are always thought provoking and worth reading and highlighting! Practice the exercises within this one and become comfortable with difficult conversations.

Switch: How to Change Things When Change Is Hard by **Chip Heath and Dan Heath** (New York: Crown Business, 2010)
A fan of their message, our coach team at Pyramid Resource Group have been highlighting successes - - "bright spots" - - in organizations for decades. I really like how these brothers and authors call attention to showcasing the good that people do every day and formalizing the approach to recognition. Celebrating contribution is a key to creating the environment for people to find their way onto the right path - - Back to the *light*.

Send us your life changing book titles by connecting with us on Facebook and through our website, Zombies to Zealots!

Soulful Gratitude

I have rarely done anything worthwhile alone. Do we ever? We aren't born without parents; we only learn in the company of others; and we can only shine in the presence of a community or audience of people who appreciate what we do.

Writing a book is an act of courage for we stand starkly exposed when we craft meaning from words. There is a vulnerability about putting thoughts to paper that is unlike any other experience in my life.

Zombies to Zealots was a message I believe is needed at this time in our evolution of work, and I sense there is a real urgency about the messages within. And because I hang out with some really cool people, I had lots of encouragers, conspirators, and champions along the way.

I hold so much compassion for those of you who choose to read this book and do the work —so the first thank you—is to YOU.

I also hold so much love for those who contributed. I especially honor all whose stories I am privileged to share. Thanks again Anne and all you wise souls and brilliant change angels and leaders.

In the conspirator line up, a *really big hug and appreciation* beyond words goes to Lynn Hays (www.Haysmar.com) for being the Sherpa guide for the initial work, both as a research partner and my first muse on this project. Your brilliant challenges, thoughts, interviews, and transcripts made Zombies possible. I wear the T-shirt!

Another really big hug goes to my family: To my business and life partner, Barry, for hauling me and the many iterations of this manuscript to the cabin and for holding possibility when I really wanted to toss it all. To Jessica for always inspiring me to play bigger and experience the world as a fearless global citizen, and to creative writer and ancient spirit muse Hank for fine tuning a few chapters and making it cool to write about such things as zombies (cause they still kinda freak me out). For my Mom for grooming the artist within me when I was a child, and to Dad for believing I was worthy of greater things than I once imagined.

For the ongoing conversation over many months to the brilliant Suzanne Murray and her colleagues, Sarah and Stefanie, at StyleMatters for developmental, style, and technical edits. YOU, dear soul, have your own stories within and I cannot wait to read them. You help writers shine through our written words.

Heartfelt gratitude wings its way to my colleagues at the Pyramid Resource Group, Inc. You are family and all contribute daily to our every creation. A special thanks goes to Barbara Poole for your help with design and your guidance throughout the change agent journey. Michele Schicchi—your encouragement and belief in my writing and in our work as coaches is a testament to the law of attraction. We must be doing something right to have found you as our Director of Business Operations. Your steady hand and willingness to take on any project—including this book—helps us grow in more ways than just the business.

A spirit-filled reverent (and, irreverent) nod goes to Jim Curtan whose language in speaking archetypes has helped me grow personally and helped define Zombies and Zealots.

And to my gal pals—for reading, cooking, laughing, and spiriting me away to more fun activities when you knew I needed them—as you always do.

About the Author

A student of the Hero's Journey, Darelyn "DJ" Mitsch has lived with one foot in the world of Spirit and one firmly planted in the world of Business – with a quiet mission to blend these often disparate worlds when coaching leaders around the globe. As an entrepreneur, DJ is focused on integral leadership, blending ancient wisdom with new technologies to more significantly engage teams for extraordinary results. In 1994 DJ founded the Pyramid Resource Group, the first corporate coaching company in the US with her partner, Barry Mitsch. Recognized as a thought leader in the coaching profession DJ was one of the first 25 business coaches in the United States to earn a Master Certified Coach designation from the International Coach Federation

(ICF) and was the organization's 6th Global President. Together she and the coaches of Pyramid Resource Group have served to develop leaders of leaders through innovative coaching programs customized to meet organizational needs of multi-national companies. DJ is the creator of the breakthrough team coaching program *Team Advantage* which unleashes teams to contribute their boldest innovations and highest team performance. For more information on that program www.Team-Advantage.com

To download the *Zombie Rescue Kit*, visit us at, www.ZombiesToZealots.com.

Endnotes

1   Amy Adkins, "U.S. Employee Engagement Reaches Three-Year High," Gallup.com, March 9, 2015, http://www.gallup.com/poll/181895/employee-engagement-reaches-three-year-high.aspx.

2   "United States Labor Force Statistics: Seasonally Adjusted (in Thousands), 1978–Present," Department of Labor Statistics, accessed December 4, 2015, http://www.dlt.ri.gov/lmi/laus/us/usadj.htm

3   Author contacted Hopi Nation for permission to use a full poem. The Elders remain unnamed - even within the nation. I used this excerpt to honor the wisdom and teachings of the Hopi - and to advance the messages of these kindred souls who are Earth's caretakers and teachers.

4   "Napoleon Hill-What the mind can conceive, believe & achieve," YouTube video, 7:01, posted by "TheUniverseWithinUs.com," October 19, 2007, https://www.youtube.com/watch?v=2hA-7aq6OXI

5   Marianne Williamson, *A Return to Love* (New York: HarperCollins, 1992), 190–91.

6   Carolyn Myss, *Sacred Contracts: Awakening Your Divine Potential* (New York: Three Rivers Press, 2002).

7   Wikipedia, s.v. Ubuntu (philosophy), last modified November 7, 2015, https://en.wikipedia.org/wiki/Ubuntu_(philosophy).

Index